Tisha's TABLE

An Eclectic Collection of Simple, *Tasty Recipes*

TISHA WYLIE

ISBN: 9781710571561

Text copyright © 2020 Tisha Wylie

Photographer: Kimi Alli

Editor: Shareen, Rivera

www.shareenrivera.com/writing-services

Family, Friends, and Food — what could be better?

I dedicate this book to my nephews, Jeremiah & Kaimani and my nieces, Tatyana, Adrea, and Mika. Auntie loves you.

My Many, Many Thanks

Thank you to my mom and dad, Barbara and Hayward Wylie, for your love and support of all my shenanigans and outspoken personality. I couldn't have done it without you.

INTRODUCTION

I love cooking. It's not a chore for me; believe it or not, I find it relaxing. I love when people enjoy the food I create, nothing gives me more satisfaction. People often ask, "How'd you come up with that?" or "Can I have that recipe?" I enjoy it even more when people take those recipes and make them their own. And thus, Tisha's Table – Creative Touch Foods was born.

I remember being a kid watching my grandma, my mom and all my aunts in the kitchen cooking. I always wanted to help; they would never let me. While still in elementary school, however, they finally allowed me in the kitchen; that was the best feeling in the world. I helped with baking pies and cakes, side dishes and on occasions, main dishes. Through the years I was able to help more and more (I think the trust factor grew). Finally, I graduated to menu planning for our Family Holiday dinners; what an honor.

People always ask me, "What style of cooking do you do?" or "What's your specialty?" and my response is always the same – "I'm a Californian Man!" I'm absolutely blessed to be a California Native. Born in Merced and raised in San Jose (about 45 minutes South of San Francisco), I've had a unique opportunity to grow up around a variety of cultures and food influences. This is certainly reflected in the recipes you will embark on in the following pages. My mother always tried different types of foods; everything from Italian influenced recipes to Indian inspired dishes. It really gave us kids a very cultured palate. I've updated some of the ingredients and made them my own.

For years, different family members and friends encouraged me to start some type of food business. I always said, "Yeah maybe someday." Well several years later, that day arrived. In 2007, I launched Tisha's Table - Creative Touch Foods. I have an opportunity to not only prepare food for people who don't have time to cook, but I'm also able to assist people who want to cook but are not always sure how. Therefore, menu planning, culinary boot camps, and cooking demos are part of my services.

For me, creating food is like creating the perfect song, gathering the right ingredients and making them somehow harmonize with each other – resulting in just the right flavor note – creating the perfect melody for people to enjoy.

As you flip through the pages of this cookbook, my hope is that you not only enjoy the recipes I've presented but allow them to also inspire you. Make them your own – or perhaps invent some original creations of your own.

The recipes are simple and tasty, so get in the kitchen and enjoy the adventure ahead.

Kitchen Organization

I believe that having a clean, organized kitchen is paramount to having a successful cooking experience. If you don't have continuous flow while you cook, it could make your time in the kitchen very challenging and more of a chore than a pleasure.

Anyone who knows me knows that I'm about all things organized. It might possibly be on the verge of crazy – but I've come to terms with it! Anyway, here are some basic things that help me while I'm in the kitchen, and some basic pantry items I like to keep on hand.

The Basics

- *Menu planning:* Whether it's just for me or whether I'm planning for a crowd, I always find it helpful to write out what I'm having for any particular meal.
- *Make a shopping list:* This will help you stay on track with what you need and it helps control impulse shopping.
- *Clean while you cook*: This will make life so much easier for you. It will eliminate the feeling of being overwhelmed with a mound of pots and pans before and after your meal. If you don't have time to clean the pots that you've used, rinse and stack them so they are more manageable when it's time to clean up.
- *Keep a clean workspace*: Spills, boil-overs, etc.
- *Try to do as much prep work as you can*: If the recipe calls for diced vegetables, try to get a head start and dice them beforehand. Gather and measure out your seasonings beforehand.

Pantry Must Haves

- Olive, Oil
- Canola Oil
- Non-Stick Spray

- Balsamic Vinegar
- Rice Vinegar
- Sesame Oil
- Kosher or sea salt
- Fresh Ground Pepper
- Red Pepper Flakes
- Garlic & Onion Powder
- Ground Cumin and Coriander
- Poultry and Steak Rub
- Chinese 5 Spice
- Spices: Ground Cinnamon, Ground Nutmeg and Ground Ginger
- Vanilla Extract and Vanilla Beans
- Chicken Stock and/or Chicken Base
- Canned Tomatoes – Crushed, Diced and Sauce
- Canned Beans: Black Beans, Kidney Beans, Chickpea, Cannellini Beans

There is much more, but these tips should get you started on your kitchen organization. Happy Cooking! ☺

CONTENTS

Tisha's
TAKE ON
"*For Starters*"

These recipes are easy to pull together, super tasty and sure to please your guest.

FOR STARTERS

Tandoori Chicken Skewers

Tomato/Basil Crostini

Plantains with Roasted Red Bell Pepper Dip

Smoked Salmon Cucumber Bites

Vegetarian Egg Rolls

Pineapple/Kiwi Salsa

Seafood-Stuffed Mushrooms

Curry Puffs

Grandma' Wylie's Crab Cakes

Spicy Chicken Wings

Savory Cheesecake Dip

Sweet Onion and Tomato Tart

Creamy White Bean Dip

Pecan Celery Sticks

Tandoori Chicken Skewers

Tandoori Chicken is so tasty. I love the spicy flavor it offers. I thought it would be a great idea to turn this meal into an appetizer. Little bite-size pieces of spicy chicken; your guests will love them.

For the chicken
2 pounds of chicken tenders
Salt and pepper to taste
12 bamboo skewers
Tandoori sauce/marinade (recipe follows)

For the Sauce/Marinade
1 tablespoon ground cumin
1 tablespoon turmeric powder

2 tablespoons coriander, ground
1 tablespoon smoky paprika
½ teaspoon ground cayenne pepper
1 jalapeño, seeded and diced
3 clove garlic
1-inch piece fresh ginger, peeled
2 cups nonfat or low-fat plain yogurt
Juice of 1 lemon
1 ½ ounce of chicken or veggie stock

For the chicken: Season chicken tenders and set aside. Soak skewers in water for about 30 minutes; set aside.

For the sauce: Place the garlic, ginger, and jalapeño in a food processor or blender and process until smooth paste forms. Add the remaining ingredients and process again until well incorporated and smooth. Pour over chicken and place in the fridge for 4 hours. Remove excess sauce/marinade and skewer the chicken tenders. Grill for about 2 minutes per side.

Tomato/Basil Crostini

The combo of the warm bread, cheese, tomato, and herb is very tasty and very satisfying. Try this recipe at your next get-together but make plenty; they go fast!

1 baguette
Olive oil
Salt and pepper to taste
1 bunch of fresh basil leaves
Grape tomatoes
Fresh mozzarella cheese, sliced

Preheat oven to 450ºF

Slice the baguette into ½ inch slices. Brush both sides with olive oil and season with salt and pepper. Bake until the slices are light brown, about 2-3 minutes. Remove from oven and add one basil leaf to each slice, one tomato half and top with the mozzarella slice. Set the oven to broil and cook for another 3 minutes or until the cheese has melted and the Crostini is golden brown.

Serve warm or at room temp.

Plantains w/ Roasted Red Pepper Dip

A year or so ago, my friend Kristina and I were driving along chatting and we started discussing plantains. I told her how I like mine and she started throwing out ideas of how she'd like to eat them. That's how this recipe came about. I tested it, and it worked. It may sound a little odd at first, but the flavors together are heavenly.

For the Plantain:
1 large plantain cut in half and sliced thin ~~and~~ lengthwise *(a ripe plantain is yellow & black)*
Salt & pepper to taste
Heavy pinch of sugar
Olive oil

For the Red Pepper Dip:
12oz jar of roasted red bell pepper, rough chopped
3oz sun-dried tomato, rough chopped
½ cup of olive oil
½ cup plain Greek yogurt
Salt & pepper to taste

Preheat oven to 400ºF

For the Plantain chips: Brush each slice with olive oil - season both sides with salt, pepper, and sugar. Transfer to a cookie sheet lined with parchment paper. Bake for about 20 minutes or until crispy (turning halfway through). Move to a serving platter.

For the Red Pepper dip: In a food processor or blender, combine the chopped red pepper, sun-dried tomato, olive oil, yogurt, salt & pepper; process until smooth. Transfer to a serving bowl and serve with the plantain chips.

Cook's Notes: If you find the dip is too thick, add the liquid from the roasted red pepper until it is the consistency you like.

Smoked Salmon Cucumber Bites

I like going to and hosting tea parties. The little bite-sized food is so cute and just right for us ladies. This is just a little different take to the regular tea sandwiches. It's healthier for you and zero carbs.

1 hothouse (or English) cucumber
8 oz of chive cream cheese, softened
4-6 oz of smoked salmon, cut into bite-size pieces
Capers, drained
Fresh dill, chopped fine for garnish

Slice the unpeeled cucumber into coins and line up on parchment paper and pat dry. For each coin, take a teaspoon of the chive cream cheese and spread evenly on the cucumber coin. Add a bite-size piece of the smoked salmon and top with a few capers and chopped dill. Repeat the process for the remaining cucumbers; stash in the fridge for about 30 minutes.

Cook's Notes: for a more elegant look, you can pipe the cream cheese onto the cucumber bites. You can also substitute cooked and peeled shrimp instead of using the smoked salmon.

Vegetarian Egg Rolls

When I was younger, my mom would make these for us kids. The thought of homemade egg rolls on Friday sent us through the roof. As we got older, we continued to make them. Here, I've updated some ingredients to give a more up-to-date flavor.

4 oz Crimini (Baby Bella) mushroom, diced fine
2 clove garlic, minced
½ small onions finely diced
6 oz of shredded carrots
6 oz of shredded Napa cabbage
¼ cup of low sodium soy sauce
1 teaspoon of ground black pepper
1 teaspoon red pepper flake (optional)
10-20 large wonton skins
Canola oil, for sauté and to fry

For the filling: In a large skillet, add 2 teaspoons of canola oil and add mushrooms and onion. Cook until soft, about 3 minutes. Add the garlic, carrots, cabbage, salt, pepper, and red pepper flakes. Continue to cook until the mixture reduces by half. Set aside to cool.

To assemble the Egg Rolls: Take a wonton skin and add two heaping tablespoons of the filling. Fold in the side of the wonton and roll starting from the side closest to you. Repeat the process until the filling is gone. In a frying pan, add enough canola oil to fill the pan with about an inch of oil. Add the egg rolls to the hot oil, cook on all sides until golden brown. Move to a wire rack to drain.

Serve warm and with your favorite dipping sauce.

Pineapple/Kiwi Salsa

Everybody knows about mango salsa, but this recipe I thought would taste good with chicken or fish. I quickly thought of things I would put into a homemade salsa and it came out great! Your guests may shy away at first, but once they have a taste they'll be hooked.

8 oz of pineapple, diced
1 large kiwi, diced
1/3 cup red onion, diced fine
½ cup cilantro, chopped fine
1 habanero OR jalapeño, seeded and diced fine
Salt & pepper to taste

In a medium-sized bowl, combine all of the above ingredients tasting for seasoning. Store in the fridge for at least ½ hour to give the flavors a chance to marinate.

Serve with tortilla chips or serve over chicken.

Seafood-Stuffed Mushrooms

My parents love seafood and they love mushrooms. I thought why not combine the two loves? I developed the recipe and presented this dish for my parents on their wedding anniversary, and it was a hit. I made extra for the rest of the family. There were no leftovers.

12 large stuffing mushrooms, stems removed
4 oz bay scallops, minced
¼ pound fresh rock shrimp, minced
Salt & pepper to taste
¼ teaspoon dry mustard
2 garlic cloves, minced fine
1 teaspoon fresh dill, minced fine
1 teaspoon fresh lemon juice
1 egg, slightly beaten
½ cup of panko bread crumbs
1 cup mozzarella, grated and divided

Preheat oven to 350ºF

Clean mushrooms and brush them with olive oil, set aside. In a bowl, mix together scallops, shrimp, salt & pepper, dry mustard, garlic, dill, and lemon juice. Add egg until well incorporated. Gently fold in panko bread crumbs. Spoon mixture into each mushroom cap. Place on cookie sheet; top each cap with the grated mozzarella. Bake for approx. 30-35 minutes or until the cheese is brown and bubbly.

Serve warm.

Curry Puffs

These little bite-sized morsels are so yummy. You will have a hard time maintaining self-control. Although this is not a traditional Indian dish, it shares the same smoky, spicy flavors; so it's a good knock off. This is an excellent starter for a meal or just for a snack.

1 pkg. of puff pastry, thawed
3-4 medium-sized potatoes, peeled and cubed
1 small onion, diced
1 tablespoon cumin seeds
Salt & pepper to taste
1 tablespoon olive oil
Egg wash (1 beaten egg + 1 tablespoon of water)

Preheat Oven to 350ºF

In a large pot, boil the cubed potatoes until tender (not mushy). Drain and add the salt & pepper; set aside. In a large skillet, heat olive oil and sauté onions for 3 minutes or until soft. Add cumin seeds and continue to cook for 1-2 more minutes or until you can smell the cumin seeds. Add the cooked potatoes to the onion/cumin seed mixture and with a fork, smash and mix the ingredients together until well incorporated. Set aside to cool.

Unfold puff pastry and separate at the seam. Take one of the pastry strips and spoon the cooled potato mixture down the middle of the strip (be sure not to overfill, otherwise, you will have trouble sealing the finished product). Take the second strip and place it on top of the first, sealing the edges with the egg wash. To vent, cut 3-4 holes on top. Brush with the egg wash. Repeat this process with remaining strips of puff pastry and potato mixture (you should end up with 3 filled pastries). Line a cookie sheet with parchment paper; bake for 25-35 minutes or until golden brown.

Cool and cut into bite-size pieces.

Grandma' Wylie's Crab Cakes

I've tasted plenty of crab cakes over the years, and I have to say that my grandmother made the best in the world. I was honored that she wanted me to carry on the legacy of this recipe. I've brought the recipe into the 21st century with some updates and a sauce addition. You'll be pleasantly surprised.

16 oz of lump crab meat
1 small onion, diced fine
2 tablespoons of light mayo
1 teaspoon of Dijon mustard
1 large egg, slightly beaten
Juice from ½ of a lemon
2-3 dashes of Worcestershire sauce

2-4 dashes of hot sauce
Heavy pinch of paprika
Salt & pepper to taste
1 cup panko bread crumbs + 1/3 for the topping
Olive oil
Italian parsley, finely chopped (optional garnish)
Curry Aioli sauce (see sauces)

In a large bowl, mix together onion, mayo, mustard, egg, lemon juice, Worcestershire sauce, hot sauce, salt & pepper, and paprika. Gingerly fold in the crab meat and panko crumbs. Form mixture into patties, top with remaining panko crumbs, and allow the patties to rest in the freezer for about 5-10 minutes. Liberally drizzle each patty with olive oil. Line a cookie sheet with parchment paper; bake in an oven preheated to 375°F and bake for 20 minutes or until they are golden brown.

Serve with Curry Aioli Sauce & garnish with chopped Italian parsley.

Spicy Chicken Wings

I created this recipe purely by accident. I was going to a tailgating party and I agreed to make the wings. The night before, I started pulling ingredients out of the fridge and pantry that I thought would taste good together. Well, they were a hit. They guys loved them and my girlfriends wanted the recipe. Make plenty of these at your next get-together – they are guaranteed to go fast.

2 pound – chicken party wings, rinsed and dried
10 oz bottle of low sodium soy sauce
1/3 cup of brown sugar
2 garlic cloves, minced
1 teaspoon grated ginger
1 teaspoon red pepper flakes
1 teaspoon sesame seed oil
½ cup cilantro, chopped
½ cup green onions, chopped (reserve some for garnish)
Toasted sesame seeds for garnish

Preheat oven to 400°F

In a large zip-top bag, combine soy sauce, brown sugar, garlic, red pepper, sesame oil, cilantro, and green onions. Whisk until well combined. Add the chicken. Put in the fridge for 1 to 2 hours. Roast in a shallow cookie sheet for 20-25 minutes.

Garnish with reserved green onion and sesame seeds.

Savory Cheesecake Dip

This recipe is a result of playing with my food. I like to entertain, so I'm always thinking of ways to do things differently, to get people's attention with my food. So I developed this unique recipe. The ingredients work well together and it's a crowd-pleaser.

8 oz sour cream
1 - 8 oz block of cream cheese, softened
2 cloves of garlic, chopped fine
1 jalapeño, seeded and chopped (for more bite, leave the seeds in)
12 oz jar roasted red bell pepper
5 oz pesto, divided (choose your favorite brand or make your own)
Salt and pepper to taste
Flat-leaf parsley, chopped for garnish

In a large bowl, mix together the sour cream, cream cheese, garlic, and jalapeño; salt and pepper to taste. Set aside.

Next, drain the roasted red bell pepper and coarsely chop them. In a 6-inch springform pan, begin to layer the ingredients in the following order: cream cheese mixture, pesto, and roasted bell pepper. Repeat the process until you come to the top layer. Sprinkle the top with chopped parsley. Cover with plastic wrap and chill for 2-3 hours or overnight

Serve with bagel chips or pita bread.

Sweet Onion and Tomato Tart

I know, I know – the thought of an onion and tomato tart sounds a little strange, but I have to say it is VERY tasty. While developing this recipe, I thought the two would work fabulously; and they did. Expand your taste buds and enjoy it.

2 large Vidalia or Spanish onion, halved & thinly sliced
Olive oil
1 tablespoon unsalted butter
Salt and pepper to taste
½ pint of yellow grape tomatoes, sliced
½ pint of red grape tomatoes, sliced
1 to 2 Tbsp of softened cream cheese
1 sheet of puff pastry, thawed
Egg wash (one whole egg + 1 tablespoon water beaten)
Shaved Parmesan cheese

Preheat oven to 425°F

To prepare the mixture: In a large preheated skillet, add the olive oil, butter, and onion, salt, and pepper to taste. Cook the onions down until they have reduced by half and they are soft and brown. Set aside to cool to room temperature. Season the tomatoes with salt and pepper and set aside.

To prepare the puff pastry: Carefully unfold the pastry (you should see two seams). Press the seams together and stretch the dough out a little. Fold up each side of the pastry about ¼ inches on all sides; brush the folded edges with the egg wash. With a fork, dock the middle of the pastry.

To assemble the tart: Transfer the prepared puff pastry to a non-stick cookie sheet. Spread a thin layer of cream cheese to the bottom of the puff pastry, then add the cooled onions to the. Next, arrange the season tomatoes on top of the onions. Bake for about 20-25 minutes or until the pastry is brown and the tomatoes are cooked through. Remove from oven and sprinkle the shaved Parmesan cheese on top and sprinkle with fresh herbs like Italian parsley.

Cut into bite sizes squares and serve.

Creamy White Bean Dip

This creamy dip is good for all occasions. It's reminiscent of hummus which is typically made with ground chickpeas. Serve with tortilla chips or for an upgrade, toasted pita triangles.

2 - 15 oz cans of cannellini beans, drained and rinsed
2 cloves garlic, peeled
1/3 cup flat-leaf parsley (plus some for garnish)
1 teaspoon red pepper flakes
¼ teaspoon ground cumin
Salt and pepper to taste
Juice ½ lemon
½ cup of olive oil
¼ cup low-fat sour cream
1/3 cup red onion, diced fine

In a food processor, add the beans, garlic, parsley, red pepper flakes, ground cumin lemon, salt & pepper, and sour cream – combine until the ingredients are well incorporated. With the processor running on low, drizzle in the olive oil and process until smooth. Transfer to a serving bowl and mix in the red onion.

Garnish with parsley, serve with toasted pita triangles.

Pecan Celery Sticks

I adore celery sticks, but I wanted to fill them with something yummy. I came up with this recipe just for my own taste buds. I shared them at an event and they were a hit, great for a nice crunchy snack.

8 stalks of celery
1 cup of toasted pecans
1 - 8oz block of cream cheese, softened
¼ cup of flat-leaf parsley
1 teaspoon roasted garlic
Salt and pepper to taste
1 teaspoon red pepper flakes (optional)

Clean and trim the celery into 3-inch pieces. Cut a small part on the bottom of each stick to create a stable surface – place the cut pieces in a bowl of cold ice water to keep them fresh and crisp, set aside. Add the toasted pecans, cream cheese, roasted garlic, salt, pepper and the red pepper flakes to a food processor. Process the ingredients until well incorporated and smooth. To create the filled sticks, fill a plastic pastry bag fitted with a 45 tip with the pecan mixture and pipe onto each celery piece. Repeat the process for the remaining ingredients. Refrigerate for 30 minutes and serve. Garnish with leftover crushed pecans or leftover chopped parsley.

Tisha's
TAKE ON
"Soups, Sandwiches and Salads"

I love the recipes in this section, very diverse in flavor. Perfect for a lazy afternoon when you don't feel like a big meal.

SOUPS, SANDWICHES, AND SALADS

Leek, Potato and Mushroom Soup

Sweet Pea and Basil Soup

Cream of Broccoli Soup

Sausage and Zucchini Soup

Roasted Butternut Squash Soup

Thai Beef Soup

Turkey and Feta Burger

Shrimp and Scallop Burger

Vietnamese Chicken Wrap

Chipotle Chicken Pita Pockets

Ham and Cheese Melt

Chinese Chicken Salad

Rigatoni and Spinach Salad

Asparagus Citrus Salad

Cucumber Feta Salad

Carrot and Cranberry Salad

Warm Bulgur Salad

Leek, Potato and Mushroom Soup

This is one of my mom's creations. I've swapped out some of the ingredients to give it a more gourmet taste. The mushrooms in this make it a little more hardy and satisfying.

½ cup pancetta, diced (see cook's note)
1 tablespoon olive oil
1 medium onion, diced
2 medium leeks, chopped and cleaned
2 clove garlic, minced
1 pound Yukon gold potatoes, diced
16 oz Crimini (Baby Bella) mushrooms, quartered

4 cups of chicken stock
1 can of evaporated milk
Salt and pepper to taste
2 tablespoon of Wondra (see cook's notes)
½ stick (4 tablespoons) unsalted butter
1/2 cup Italian Parsley, chopped plus some for garnish

In a large pot, add olive oil and pancetta; cook for about 3 minutes. Add the onion and leeks; cook for another 5-10 minutes or until the onions are soft. Add the garlic, potatoes, and mushrooms; continue to cook for another 2-3 minutes. Salt and pepper to taste. Add the chicken stock and milk. Simmer for 20 minutes. Add the Wondra, parsley, and butter. Simmer for an additional 10 minutes

Garnish with parsley and serve.

Cook's Notes: The pancetta has plenty of salt for the whole dish. But if you find that you need more salt, go easy. Wondra is super fine flour. If you don't have or cannot find it, no worries, just use regular flour.

Creamy Sweet Pea and Basil Soup

The inspiration for this soup came when I had to complete a project for one of my culinary classes – I needed to create a soup dish for the menu – and this creamy soup was born. All have to say, the Chef Instructor was impressed.

1 - 16 oz pkg frozen sweet peas
1 small onion, diced
1 garlic clove, minced
2 tablespoon olive oil
3 cups chicken stock
15 Basil leaves, roughly chopped
Salt and pepper to taste
Sour cream and an extra basil leaf for garnish

In a medium pot, bring the chicken stock to a simmer to keep it warm. Heat a large skillet to medium-high; add the olive oil and onion. Cook for about 2 minutes or until the onions are soft; add the garlic and the sweet peas. Continue to cook until the peas are completely cooked through. Add the hot peas and basil leaves to a food processor. While the processor is on, slowly add the warm chicken stock to the pea and basil mixture via the food processor fed tube (you may need to do this in two batches).

Transfer the soup to the individual soup bowls and garnish with a dollop of sour cream and basil leaf.

Cream of Broccoli Soup

I really enjoy the cream of broccoli; that my mom made for us kids back in the day. So I wanted to dedicate this recipe to her. Hope I do you proud, mom.

1 medium onion, diced
2-3 cloves garlic, minced
2 tablespoons olive oil
3 cups broccoli florets
5 cups chicken broth
1 ½ cup milk
Salt and pepper to taste
½ cup Parmesan cheese, grated

In a large pot, add the onion and olive oil; cook for about 3-5 minutes. Add the garlic and the broccoli. Continue to cook for another 5 minutes (add a little more olive oil if the pot becomes too dry). Salt and pepper to taste. Add the chicken broth and milk. Simmer on low for 20 minutes. Stir in the Parmesan cheese and serve.

Sausage & Zucchini Soup

This soup is good at any time, trust me. It will wrap its arms around you and won't let go. And because I use fresh veggies and turkey sausage, it's good for your health too.

1 medium onion, diced
2 garlic cloves, minced
2 scallions, cleaned and chopped
Olive oil
Salt and pepper
1 teaspoon of red pepper flakes
4 mild turkey sausages
4 spicy turkey sausages
2 large zucchini, cut into half-moon shapes
One 28 oz can of diced tomatoes
6 cups of chicken stock
1-½ cups of cooked rice
½ cup of Italian parsley

In a hot skillet, brown the sausages on both sides – about 2 minutes per side – then cut them into coin size pieces.

In a large pot, add olive oil (enough to coat the bottom of the pot), onion, and scallion; cook for about 3 minutes or until the onions become soft. Add the sausage, zucchini, diced tomatoes, and garlic; continue to cook for another 5 minutes. Season with salt, pepper, and red pepper flakes. Finally, add the chicken stock. Cover and bring to a boil for 3 minutes. Simmer for 25 minutes. Add the cooked rice and Italian parsley; simmer for an additional 5 minutes.

Serve hot with crusty bread.

Roasted Butternut Squash Soup

This soup is creamy, velvety, filling, and will warm the soul. Who says this soup has to be seasonal? Enjoy.

1 large onion, rough chopped
3 large carrots, cleaned and cut into small pieces
1 large butternut squash, peeled, seeded and cut into cubes
2 garlic cloves, peeled and smashed
Salt and pepper to taste
Olive oil
2 sprigs of fresh thyme
2 fresh sage leaves or 1 teaspoon ground sage
4 cups of chicken or vegetable stock
1 cup of milk or heavy cream
2 tablespoons of butter

Preheat oven to 400°F

In a roasting pan, add the onion, carrots, butternut squash, and garlic; season with salt and pepper. Add the thyme and sage and drizzle with olive oil. Roast in the oven for 30 to 40 minutes or until the squash and carrots are tender and perfectly roasted. Remove the thyme stems and discard.

To a large pot, add the roasted vegetables and chicken stock – add more salt and pepper if needed. Simmer for about 15 minutes.

With your emersion stick blender, blend the ingredients until smooth. Add milk and butter and stir until smooth and velvety.

Garnish with sour cream and serve immediately.

Cook's Notes: For the adventurous cook, try replacing the milk or cream with coconut milk for a more exotic taste.

Thai Beef Soup

I really enjoy Thai food. I love the spicy flavors offered in this dish. Here, I've taken some typical Thai flavors and added them to a flavorful broth.

6 cups of beef stock
3 coins of fresh ginger, peeled
2 cloves garlic, minced
1 stalk of lemongrass, halved and crushed
8 oz of shitake mushrooms, sliced
1-2 baby bok choy, chopped
2 fresh red chili peppers, rough chopped
1 lb. London broil, sliced thin
½ teaspoon lime zest & juice of ½ limes
Salt and pepper to taste
¾ cup of coconut milk
Shredded carrot and sliced scallion for garnish

In a medium pot, add the beef stock, ginger, garlic, lemongrass, and mushrooms. Simmer on medium-low heat for about 15 minutes. Add the bok choy, red chili, beef, lime zest & juice; salt and pepper to taste. Stir well and bring to boil for 3 minutes. Reduce heat to medium-low and simmer for an additional 10-15 minutes or until the beef is done and vegetables are tender. Stir in coconut milk.

Garnish with carrot and sliced scallion.

Turkey Feta Burger

I love the little surprise in the middle of these burgers and so will your guests! In this recipe, I use ground turkey to keep it on the healthy side.

1 pound of ground turkey
1 egg, slightly beaten
¼ cup sour cream
4 dashes of Worcestershire sauce
¼ cup of grated onion
1 teaspoon salt
½ teaspoon pepper

1 teaspoon garlic powder
Pinch of red pepper flakes
4-6 oz garlic/herb feta cheese
Olive oil
3 Kaiser rolls
Sweet & Spicy Sauce (see sauces)

In a large bowl, combine the ground turkey, Worcestershire sauce, onion, salt, pepper, garlic powder, and red pepper flakes; mix until the ingredients are well incorporated. Divide the mixture into three large balls. Take one of the balls and divide in half to make two patties. Take one of the patties and spoon one heaping teaspoon of the feta in the middle of the patty; top with the remaining patty, sealing the edges all the way around. Repeat this process with the remaining meatballs. Drizzle with olive oil and transfer the filled patties to the grill and cook for about 15 minutes or until the patties are done.

Serve with the sweet and spicy sauce on warm Kaiser Rolls.

Cook's Notes: Want to try another cheese? Provolone or bleu cheese works great too. You can also grill these indoors or outdoors for even more flavor.

Shrimp and Scallop Burger

I tested this recipe out on my mom; she loved it, so naturally, I would share it with you. This is a great burger for non-meat eaters and meat-eaters alike, a unique twist on a traditional burger.

1 lb. bay scallops (small ones), rinsed and minced
1 lb. medium shrimp, cleaned, shelled and minced
½ teaspoon of each: salt, pepper, Dijon mustard
1 large shallot, grated
Juice of 1 lemon
½ cup Greek yogurt
¼ cup Italian parsley, finely chopped
1 egg
1/3 cup panko crumbs

In a large bowl, combine the minced scallops, shrimp, salt, and pepper, and mustard, shallot, and lemon juice – mix well. Add the remaining ingredients: yogurt, parsley, egg and panko crumbs – mix until well combined. Form into burgers and place on parchment paper; refrigerate for at least one hour. Spray a skillet with non-stick cooking spray (be generous); heat to medium heat, and cook burgers about 3 – 5 minutes per side depending on the thickness and until done.

Cook's Note: Serve on a Kaiser roll with your favorite chutney.

Vietnamese Chicken Wrap

I love the fresh taste of spring rolls, but sometimes they leave me feeling a little empty. So I took some of those same flavors came up with this more filling and healthy version of the spring roll and I put it in a wrap; very tasty and very satisfying.

3 chicken breasts, cooked and cut into
   ½ inch strips
3 oz shitake mushrooms, sliced and divided
3 oz carrots, sliced thin
3 oz hothouse cucumber, sliced thin
¾ cup of rice noodles
2 green onions cut in half and sliced
   lengthwise

4-6 sprigs of cilantro, divided
2 tablespoons mint leaves, rough chopped
4 cups of arugula, divided
4 Tomato/Herb wraps
Olive oil
Salt and pepper
Peanut sauce (see sauces)

Place rice noodles in a large bowl and cover with boiling water, allow to sit for about 10 minutes or until noodles are soft. Drain and set noodles aside.

To assemble the wraps: take a wrap and lay down one cup of arugula. Drizzle with olive oil plus salt and pepper to taste. Next, add 3-4 strips of the cooked chicken, 3-4 slices of the mushroom, the carrot, cucumber, and rice noodles. Finally add a few sprigs of cilantro, a pinch of mint leaves and the green onion. Top the whole thing with the peanut sauce. 'Wrap' everything together similar to wrapping a burrito. Slice in half and serve. Repeat the process for the remaining ingredients.

Chipotle Chicken Pita Pockets

The inspiration for this came from a fast food joint, believe it or not. They made a salad out of some of these ingredients and I deiced that those same ingredients would taste great in a pita. The sauce is what makes this whole thing rock.

3 Boneless chicken breasts
Salt, pepper, and garlic powder to taste
2 green onions, chopped
1 jalapeño, seeded and diced fine
½ cup shredded pepper jack cheese
2-4 small pita pockets
Chipotle sauce (see sauces)

Season the chicken with salt, pepper, and garlic powder and grill until done. Cube chicken and set aside. In a large bowl add the cubed chicken, green onions, jalapeño, cheese, lettuce, and chipotle sauce. Mix until all ingredients are combined and are evenly distributed throughout the sauce.

Fill each pita with the chicken mixture and serve.

Crunchy Ham and Cheese Melt

Some years ago, my brother was working at a deli and he introduced me to Havarti cheese. It is so creamy and yummy. I thought it would go perfectly in a sandwich. Serve with soup or a side salad. Mmmm tasty.

8 slices of sourdough bread, divided
8 slices of Havarti cheese, 1/2 inch thick, divided
8 slices of smoked ham, ¼ inch thick, divided
1 apple, thinly sliced and divided
Olive oil
4 pats of unsalted butter

Preheat griddle to 350°F

Brush the slices of bread with olive oil. To build the sandwich, add a slice of cheese to the bottom slice of bread; add two slices of ham, another slice of cheese, and finally, a few slices of apple. Top with the other slice of bread. Repeat this process with the remaining ingredients. Add butter to the griddle and cook sandwiches until golden brown and cheese is melted.

Serve immediately.

Chinese Chicken Salad

For me, this salad is so refreshing. It's certainly a meal all by itself. The fresh cilantro gives this salad a very bold fresh taste.

For the salad:
2 cup of iceberg lettuce, shredded
1 cup of Napa cabbage, shredded
½ cup of cilantro, chopped
2 cups of cooked chicken breast, shredded
1/3 cup sliced almonds
10 mandarin orange segments
Rice Wine Vinaigrette (recipe follows)

For the Vinaigrette:
¾ cup of rice wine vinegar
3 tablespoon sesame oil
Heavy pinch of Salt & Pepper
½ teaspoon red pepper flakes

In a large bowl, combine the lettuce, cabbage, cilantro, chicken, peanuts and mandarin orange segments. Lightly toss the ingredients until well incorporated. Dress with the rice wine vinaigrette.

Rigatoni Spinach Salad

In this salad, you get it all: protein, veggies and some carbs. This salad is very satisfying, and filling; great for entertaining.

1 lb. rigatoni pasta
8-10 strips of turkey bacon
5 oz feta cheese
1 small red onion, diced fine
10 oz baby spinach leaves
Zest of 1 lemon
Juice of 1 lemon
½ cup champagne vinegar
¾ cup olive oil
Salt and Pepper to taste

Cook bacon until crispy; crumble and set aside. Cook pasta according to the box directions. Drain, add salt and pepper and transfer to a large bowl. To the warm pasta, add the crumbled turkey bacon, feta cheese, diced red onion, and spinach. Check for seasoning and add more salt and pepper if needed. In a small bowl, combine the lemon zest, lemon juice, champagne vinegar, and olive oil; whisk until the ingredients are well incorporated. Salt and pepper to taste. Pour over the pasta mixture and toss until everything is well coated.

Serve immediately.

Cook's Note: You can substitute the turkey bacon with pancetta, regular pork bacon, strips of chicken, steak or even fish.

Asparagus Citrus Salad

You will enjoy this fresh, tangy salad. Good as a side dish or as a light lunch.

1 lb. fresh asparagus*, cleaned and trimmed
Salt and pepper to taste
1 large ruby red grapefruit, peeled and sectioned
2 Blood oranges, peeled and sectioned
Zest of 1 lemon
Salt and pepper
3 mint leaves
Citrus vinaigrette (see sauces and dressing section)

Bring a large pot of water to a boil. Add 1 teaspoon of salt and the trimmed asparagus to the boiling water. Allow the asparagus to blanch for 2-3 minutes, or until they are bright green and pliable. Immediately transfer them to a cold-water bath to halt the cooking; move to a mixing bowl and season with salt and pepper. Add the grapefruit, blood orange, lemon zest, and mint leaves – mix gently. Add the vinaigrette and mix again until all ingredients are well combined.

Cook's Notes: If fresh asparagus are not readily available, you can use frozen asparagus spears, and the dish will still taste great. ***do not use canned asparagus***

Cucumber and Feta Salad

I really like English or hothouse cucumbers. They have fewer seeds than the other and because it is wrapped in plastic, you don't get that filmy wax like the other. I've made this salad a million times and it is always tasty and refreshing. Good for lunch or as a side dish.

1 English cucumber
2 oz of fresh feta cheese
½ cup red onion diced fine
½ cup toasted walnut halves
2 mint leaves, cut into thin strips
½ teaspoon fresh dill
½ cup olive oil
½ teaspoon lemon zest
Juice of one lemon
Salt and pepper to taste

In a bowl, mix together the cucumber, feta, red onion, walnuts, mint and the dill – salt and pepper to taste. Feta is very salty so go easy when adding extra salt to this dish.

In a small bowl, combine olive oil, lemon zest, and lemon juice – salt and pepper to taste; whisk together and pour over the cucumber mixture. Set in the fridge for at least 30 minutes.

Serve cold or at room temp.

Carrot and Cranberry Salad

This dish is tasty all by itself or as a side dish for your lunch or dinner. I love the sweet and tangy combo of all of the ingredients.

3 medium carrots
½ cup dried cranberries
¾ cup canned pineapple tidbits, drained well
1 teaspoon lemon zest
Juice from half a lemon
2 tablespoons of light mayo
1 tablespoon of light sour cream
Salt and pepper to taste

Clean and dry carrots. With a vegetable peeler, peel the carrot lengthwise creating long ribbons of carrot; transfer to a bowl. Add the dried cranberries, pineapple tidbits, and lemon zest – salt and pepper to taste. In a separate bowl, combine lemon juice, mayo, and sour cream. Mix well and add to the carrot and fruit mixture. Chill for at least 1 hour.

Cook's Notes: You can substitute raisins for cranberries.

Warm Bulgur Salad

This dish is healthy and tasty; it's a great side dish and a wonderful way to get healthy grains into your system.

2 cups cooked bulgur, warm
1 teaspoon red wine vinegar
½ cup green and black olives cut lengthwise
½ cup peas, defrosted
1 zucchini, diced
½ cup red onion, diced
Salt and pepper to taste
½ teaspoon of red pepper flakes
Olive oil

In a medium skillet, add the olive oil, red onion, zucchini, peas, and olives. Cook for about 3-5 minutes or until the veggies are soft and warm. Add the vinegar, red pepper flakes and veggie mixture to the warm bulgur – salt and pepper to taste. Mix until all of the ingredients are well combined. Drizzle with olive oil.

Serve warm or at room temp.

Tisha's
TAKE ON
"Dinner Time"

Who doesn't love dinner time? These recipes have a little something for everyone's taste buds. Try one or two, or try them all! You won't be disappointed.

DINNER TIME (POULTRY, SEAFOOD, BEEF, PORK & LAMB)

Panko Crusted Chicken in a Mustard Sauce

Chicken in a Garlic Chili Sauce

Chicken in a Tangy Pom Sauce

Linguine with Chicken and Mushrooms

Pappardelle Toss

Firecracker Penne with Turkey Cutlets

Mom's Stuffed Peppers

Rockfish Wrapped in Crispy Pancetta

Seared Chilean Sea Bass

Halibut Wrapped in Phyllo

Lobster Spaghetti

Grilled Shrimp in a Zesty Orange Balsamic Glaze

Shrimp n' Chicken Sausage in a Creamy Dill Sauce

Beef Stroganoff

Beef Braciole in a Spicy Tomato Sauce

Stuffed Pork Chops

Curried Pork Spareribs

5-Spice Pork Shoulder

Braised Lamb Chops

Panko Crusted Chicken in a Mustard Sauce

Our family eats a lot of chicken, what American doesn't? But it can sometimes get boring. This recipe was a result of a pantry raid. The crunchy panko gives this dish an extra special flavor.

4 boneless, skinless chicken breasts
Salt & pepper to taste
½ teaspoon of onion powder
½ teaspoon of garlic powder
¼ teaspoon of cayenne pepper
½ cup flour
1 egg, slightly beaten
1 ½ cup of panko crumbs
Olive oil, enough to coat the bottom of the pan
Mustard Sauce (see sauces)

For the chicken: butterfly each chicken breast. With a meat mallet, pound each one out to about ¼ inch thick. Season with salt, pepper, onion, garlic powder and cayenne. Lightly flour the chicken, and roll it in the beaten egg. Finally, coat with the panko crumbs making sure to press the panko into the chicken. Coat a non-stick skillet with olive oil and cook each breast for about 4 – 5 minutes per side or until done. Serve with mustard sauce and hot buttered noodles.

Chicken in a Garlic Chili Sauce

This dish is spicy and super delicious. The chicken thighs give a rich flavor and the chili garlic paste gives it a spicy kick.

10 boneless/skinless chicken thighs
1 tablespoon of olive oil
½ teaspoon salt
1 teaspoon pepper
1 teaspoon garlic powder
½ cup low sodium soy sauce
2 tablespoons chili garlic paste
¾ cup of warm water
1 teaspoon sesame seeds

In a small bowl, whisk together the soy sauce, chili garlic paste, and water and set aside. Season both sides of the chicken with the salt, pepper and garlic powder. In a large preheated skillet, add the olive oil and chicken thighs; brown on both sides (about 1 minute per side). Add the soy sauce mixture to the skillet. Cover and simmer for 15-20 minutes or until the chicken is cooked all the way through. Sprinkle with the sesame seeds and serve with brown rice.

Cook's Notes: You can also do this with boneless/skinless chicken breast or salmon pieces. The only difference is that you will simmer for 10-15 minutes instead of the 15-20.

Chicken in a Tangy Pom Sauce

I know the combination of chicken and pomegranate sounds really strange, but once you taste this, you'll understand why this recipe is so popular with my family and friends.

2 - 6 oz. bone-in chicken breast
Salt & pepper to taste
Onion powder to taste
1 cup of pomegranate molasses
1 teaspoon of olive oil
1 pat of unsalted butter
Pomegranate seeds for garnish

For the Chicken: Season chicken with salt, pepper & onion powder. Roast in the oven preheated to 400°F for about 45 minutes. Set aside in a warm place.

For the sauce: In a saucepan, add olive oil and pomegranate molasses. On medium heat, cook for about 2 minutes until completely warmed through. Stir in the pat of butter and brush liberally over chicken breast.

Cook's Note: Want to use something other than chicken? You can also use boneless pork chops instead of chicken in this recipe.

Linguine with Chicken and Mushrooms

The combination of tender chicken and firm meaty crimini mushroom – also called baby Bellas, will make your tummy smile.

1.5 lbs. chicken tenders
Salt & pepper to taste
Olive oil
2 Clove garlic smashed
1 Small onion, small diced
1 cup of dry white wine
2 Pats of butter
½ cup Italian parsley chopped fine
16 oz. crimini mushrooms, cleaned and quartered
1 lb. of linguine pasta (reserve ½ cup of the pasta water)

Cook pasta according to box directions, remembering to add a heavy dose of salt to the boiling water before adding the pasta. Drizzle chicken tenders with olive oil. Salt and pepper and brown on both sides in a hot skillet, about 2 minutes. Remove the tenders from the pan and set aside. Add a little more olive oil and add the diced onions, garlic and mushrooms to the pan; cook for about 5 minutes or until mushrooms are soft. Add the white wine, parsley, and reserved pasta water; return the chicken strips to the sauce and simmer on low until the chicken is done about 10 minutes. Drain pasta and add to a large serving dish. Pour the chicken/mushroom mixture over the pasta. Garnish with some chopped parsley.

Cook's Note: for a creamy sauce, you can add ½ cup of sour cream or plain Greek yogurt to the chicken/ mushroom mixture before pouring over the pasta.

Pappardelle Toss

This is a great pasta to play around with. It's soft in texture but works well with my ingredient list below.

12 oz. Pappardelle pasta
2 large zucchini, sliced into thin strips
1 small red onion
1 small shallot, minced
2 garlic cloves minced
1 lb. turkey kielbasa, cut into short strips
¼ cup olive oil
1 teaspoon red pepper flakes
Salt and pepper to taste
2 tablespoons of butter
Zest of one lemon
Juice of one lemon
¼ cup of Italian parsley
Shaved Parmesan cheese

Prepare the Pappardelle according to package directions, reserving 1-2 cups of the pasta water. In a large skillet, add the olive oil, kielbasa, red onion, shallot, and garlic; cook for about 5 minutes. Add the zucchini and continue to cook for an additional 3 minutes; salt and pepper to taste. Add the drained pasta, pasta water, butter, lemon juice, lemon zest, and parsley. Toss together until all ingredients are well incorporated. Top with Parmesan cheese and serve.

Cook's Notes: Pappardelle is egg pasta, much like egg noodles. You can find it in most specialty stores like Trader Joe's or Whole Foods. If you cannot find it, just substitute it with linguine or fettuccine.

Firecracker Penne with Turkey Cutlets

I am a fan of spicy food. This recipe will satisfy your love of cheese, spice, and pasta. Yummy!

1 pound penne pasta
Olive oil
2 Roma tomatoes, seeded and diced
¼ cup fresh jalapeños, diced (plus some for garnish)
3- 4 turkey cutlets
Salt and pepper to taste

Spicy Alfredo Sauce
1 cup unsalted butter
3 cloves garlic, minced
3 cups heavy cream
½ cup of chicken stock
1 heavy teaspoon of cayenne pepper
Pinch of salt
2 cups Parmesan cheese
1 ½ cups cheddar cheese, shredded

Cook the pasta according to package directions. Drain, drizzle with olive oil and season with salt and pepper. Mix in the Roma tomatoes and jalapeños; set aside. Meanwhile, season the turkey with salt and pepper, grill until done, and cut into bite-size pieces; add to the pasta tomato mixture.

For the spicy Alfredo sauce: in a separate saucepan, melt the butter over medium-low heat. Add the garlic, heavy cream, chicken stock, cayenne pepper, and salt; bring to a simmer. When the mixture has reached a soft boil, reduce heat down to low. Stir in the Parmesan cheese and simmer for 5-8 minutes. Pour the Alfredo sauce over the chicken and pasta mixture until well combined. Sprinkle the cheddar cheese over the entire dish and broil in the oven until the cheddar cheese has just melted.

Garnish with Italian parsley and jalapeños; serve immediately.

Mom's Stuffed Peppers

This was an old staple in our house when we were younger. It was a very sneaky way to get us to eat bell peppers. Now every time I make these, it takes me back to when I was a kid.

3 medium bell peppers (red, green, yellow or orange)
Olive oil
1pound ground turkey
1 ½ cups cooked wild rice
Salt & pepper to taste
½ teaspoon red pepper flake (optional)
½ onion, grated
2 cloves of garlic, minced
½ cup Italian parsley, minced
1 egg, slightly beaten
1 ½ cup of panko bread crumbs, divided
28 oz. jar of your favorite marinara sauce

Preheat the oven to 375°F

For the peppers: Cut each bell pepper in half lengthwise. You should end up with 6 halves. Seed and remove the white ribs from each bell. Brush inside and out with olive oil. Set aside.

For the filling: Using your hands (I know what you're thinking, but they are a Cook's best tool), combine ground meat, brown rice, salt, pepper, red pepper flakes, onion, garlic, parsley, and egg until all ingredients are well incorporated. Finally, fold in one cup of the panko bread crumbs. Fill each bell pepper cup with the meat & rice mixture and top each with the remaining panko bread crumbs. Place the filled peppers in a casserole dish and add the marinara sauce. Drizzle each cup with olive oil. Bake for 45 minutes or until filling is done.

Serve warm.

Rockfish Wrapped in Crispy Pancetta

Rockfish are very tasty. It's delicate and mild in flavor. The combination of the whitefish and the salty pancetta is a pleasant surprise.

2 Rockfish fillets
8 strips of pancetta
½ onion, sliced into thin half-moons
Pepper to taste
Garlic powder to taste
Red pepper flakes
Olive oil
Non-Stick spray
Chopped Italian parsley for garnish

Cut each fillet in half – you will end up with 4 pieces of fish. Lightly coat the fish with olive oil and liberally season both sides with pepper, garlic powder, and red pepper flakes. Take one strip of pancetta and wrap the fish; repeat with the second strip of pancetta and set aside. Repeat the process with the remaining fish. In a hot oven-proof skillet sprayed with non-stick spray, place each piece of fish into the hot skillet; sear on both sides for about 1-2 minutes. Place in the oven and broil for an additional 10-12 minutes, or until the fish begins to flake and the pancetta is crispy.
Squeeze lemon on top of the fish, garnish with chopped Italian parsley - serve with buttered rice or pasta

Cook's Note: The pancetta is very salty so in this recipe I omitted the salt. Also, if you want to keep it on the healthier side, you can use turkey bacon.

Seared Chilean Sea Bass with Mango/Cranberry Salsa

C hilean sea bass is meaty yet delicate. It pairs very well with the salsa.

2 Chilean sea bass fillets
Salt, pepper, and garlic powder to taste
Olive oil

For the Salsa
2 firm, but ripe mangos, diced small
¼ cup dried cranberries
1 large garlic clove, minced
½ cup red onion, diced
¼ cup cilantro, chopped fine
1 Serrano chili pepper, seeded and diced fine
Zest and juice of 2 limes
Salt and pepper to taste

Spray a cast-iron skillet with non-stick spray and heat to medium heat for 3 minutes or so. While your skillet is preheating, lightly coat the fish with olive oil and season with the salt, pepper and garlic powder. Sear the fish skin side down for 3 minutes and flip and cook for an additional 3-5 minutes or until the fish is cooked all the way through. Top with the homemade salsa.

For the salsa: Combined all of the ingredients in a medium bowl and mix well. Stash in the fridge for a few hours.

Cook's Note: If you cannot find Chilean sea bass, you can use snapper as a replacement.

Halibut Wrapped in Phyllo

Halibut is a nice firm white fish. Perfect for baking in phyllo dough. The tender fish inside and crunchy, buttery, flaky dough on the outside. A great date night dinner.

2 halibut fillets
Basil oil (recipes follows)
Salt and pepper to taste
Zest from 1 lemon
1 small shallot, diced fine
2 garlic cloves, diced
10 sheets of phyllo dough

Basil Oil
2 cups of olive oil
10-12 basil leaves
To a medium saucepan, add the oil and basil leaves. Slowly warm on medium-low heat until completely warmed through. Remove from heat and set aside allowing the basil to infuse in the oil. Cool completely. Remove basil leaves and store them at room temp. This can be made the day before.

Preheat oven to 400°F

Salt and pepper the fillets; set aside. Take the phyllo dough and lay the sheets down on a clean dry surface. With a paring knife, cut the dough down the middle. You should now have 2 halves with 10 sheets of dough. Take one half of the dough and brush with the basil oil and place the fish in the middle. Top with lemon zest, shallot, and garlic. Wrap the fish securely in the dough and place it on a cookie sheet lined with parchment paper. Brush the top with more basil oil. Repeat this process for the second fillet. Bake until golden brown and puffy, about 25 minutes.

Cook's Note: Garnish with sour cream and ribbons of fresh basil

Lobster Spaghetti

Nowadays, lobster is considered to be a luxury item. But if you play your cards right, you can have a delicious lobster dinner that won't break the bank and will satisfy your belly.

2 - 8oz lobster tails, removed from the shell and cut into coins
½ cup frozen peas
Salt and pepper to taste
Zest and juice from 1 lemon
Olive oil
2 garlic cloves, diced and divided
2 pats of butter, divided
Red pepper flakes (optional)
½ lbs. of spaghetti
Italian parsley, chopped (optional garnish)

Cook spaghetti according to package directions. Drain, making sure to reserve a cup of pasta water. Drizzle pasta with olive oil, one pat of butter, salt and pepper, garlic and red pepper flakes. Add a small amount of the pasta water to keep the pasta separated (this will also make a little sauce). Set aside.

In a medium skillet, heat the olive oil and peas. Cook for about 2 minutes to warm up the peas. Add the lobster coins, salt, and pepper to the skillet. Cook until the lobster meat is opaque and red on the outside. Add the remaining butter, lemon zest, lemon juice and a small amount of pasta water to create a sauce. Serve over the pasta and garnish with chopped Italian parsley.

Cook's Note: If you don't care for peas, you can substitute with diced green peppers.

Grilled Shrimp in a Zesty Orange Balsamic Glaze

My family loves seafood, so I'm always looking for different flavor combinations to satisfy the seafood craving and to get away from the same ol' same ol'. The fresh taste of the orange and the distinct taste of the balsamic make this a great combination of flavors.

1 lb. large shrimp, cleaned and deveined
2 tablespoons of olive oil
Salt & pepper to taste
½ teaspoon red pepper flakes
1 cup of balsamic vinegar
1 clove garlic, finely minced
1 teaspoon shallot, finely minced
1 teaspoon orange zest (+ some for garnish)

For the Balsamic Glaze: In a small saucepan, add the vinegar, garlic, shallot, and orange zest. Stir until combined. Salt & pepper to taste. Cook until the mixture has reduced by half. The mixture should be thick and syrup-like. Set aside.

For the Shrimp: Preheat grill pan. In a medium bowl, mix shrimp with olive oil, salt, pepper, and red pepper flakes. Grill shrimp for 2 to 3 minutes or until they are pink and firm. Drizzle the shrimp with the balsamic glaze (the glaze is strong; a little goes a long way).

Serve with orange-scented jasmine rice, garnish with orange zest and sesame seeds.

Shrimp n' Chicken Sausage in a Creamy Dill Sauce

I love the tender shrimp and the plump sausage in the creamy dill sauce. You'll find that the Orecchiette pasta is the perfect shape to hold the yummy sauce.

½ lbs. large shrimp, shelled, cleaned and deveined
4 chicken sausages cut into coins
1 lb. Orecchiette pasta
Olive oil
Salt and pepper to taste

For the dill sauce:
1 tablespoon fresh dill, chopped fine
1 tablespoon olive oil
1 tablespoon all-purpose flour
1 cup of milk or cream
½ cup Parmesan cheese

Cook Orecchiette pasta according to box directions, remembering to add a heavy dose of salt to the boiling water before adding the pasta. In a large skillet, drizzle with olive oil and add the sausage coins; cook for 3- 5 minutes. Add the shrimp and continue to cook until shrimp are pink and opaque and the sausage is done. Remove from the pan and set aside.

For the dill sauce: Working in the same pan, add the olive oil and flour. Whisk until the flour and oil until combined; salt and pepper to taste. Slowly add the milk until the mixture becomes thick. Turn off the heat and add the fresh dill and Parmesan cheese. Add the shrimp and chicken back to the pan and mix until well coated. Pour sauce on top of the cooked pasta and serve.

Cook's note: If you cannot find Orecchiette pasta, you can use penne or rigatoni.

Beef Stroganoff

This dish is a childhood favorite of mine. My mom made it for us kids often. In this recipe, I use the freshest ingredients possible. No prepackage stuff here.

2 lbs. London broil steak, cut into thin strips
1 medium onion, diced
2 clove garlic, minced
16 oz Crimini (baby Bellas) mushrooms, quartered
Olive oil (save 3 tbsp. for the roux)
3 tbsp. flour
4 cups beef stock
8 oz sour cream
1 lb. cooked egg noodles
2 pats of butter
¼ cup of Italian parsley, chopped fine
Salt and pepper to taste

In a large preheated skillet, add the olive oil and strips of beef; salt and pepper to taste. Brown the meat for about 2-3 minutes and remove from the skillet. Next, add the diced onions and mushrooms (add more olive oil if the pan becomes dry). Continue to cook until mushrooms and onions are soft. Add garlic to the pan. Push the mushroom and onion mixture to one side and stir in the flour and 3 tablespoons of olive oil. Cook for 1-2 minutes. Add the beef broth and whisk until there are no lumps. Return the browned beef to the skillet, and simmer the meat and mushroom/onion mixture for 10-15 minutes. Remove from heat and stir in the sour cream and flat-leaf parsley.

For the noodles: Cook according to package directions; drain cooked noodles thoroughly. Salt and pepper to taste and add the 2 pats of butter. Mix until well combined and butter has melted.

Serve immediately.

Beef Braciole in a Spicy Tomato Sauce

This dish is easy and delicious. Who doesn't like rolled meat stuffed with stuff? It's great for entertaining because you can make it ahead. Try mixing up the cheeses for a different flavor combination.

8 slices of thin cut beef
8 slices of provolone cheese
8 thick strips of roasted red bell pepper
8 large fresh basil leaves
Salt and pepper to taste
Olive oil
1 - 28oz can crushed tomatoes
1 tablespoon tomato paste

2 garlic cloves
1 teaspoon of dried oregano
3 thyme sprigs
½ small onion, grated
Salt and pepper to taste
¼ to 1 teaspoon of red pepper flakes (add more or less depending on how spicy you want it)

Season the meat on both sides. On top of one of the beef slices, lay a slice of cheese, a strip of roasted red pepper down the middle, and finally a basil leaf. Roll and secure with a couple of toothpicks. Repeat until you have 8 Braciole. Coat the bottom of a large skillet with olive oil, heat to medium-high and brown the Braciole on all sides; remove from pan. To the same skillet, add more olive oil if needed, the onion, garlic, and thyme. Cook for about 3 minutes. Add the crushed tomato and tomato paste; stir until well combined. Add the red pepper flakes and return the Braciole to the sauce. Turn the skillet down to low and simmer for 15-20 minutes or until hot and bubbly.

Serve immediately with rice or your favorite pasta.

Cook's Notes: You can use any good melting cheese. Swiss, Fontina or even Gorgonzola.

Stuffed Pork Chops

I enjoy stuffed pork chops... stuffed anything really. But you typically end up with lots of starchy filling, which is not good for you. In this recipe, you'll get nothing but the fresh taste of spinach, mushroom, herbs, and cheese. Your waistline will thank you.

4 oz tomato/basil feta cheese

For the filling:

For the chops:

1 tablespoon olive oil
5 oz fresh baby spinach
4 oz of mushrooms, chopped
2 garlic cloves, minced
½ cup Italian parsley, chopped

4 large pork chops, boneless
Salt and pepper to taste
Garlic powder
1 tablespoon olive oil
Toothpicks

Preheat oven to 375°F

For the filling: In a large hot skillet, add olive oil and mushrooms; cook for 3 minutes. Add the spinach, garlic, parsley and salt and pepper to taste. Cook until the spinach has wilted down. Drain the excess liquid. Transfer to a bowl and add the feta. Set aside to cool completely.

For the chops: Take each pork chop and cut open lengthwise like a book (do not cut all the way through, leave the meat attached towards the end). Season both sides with salt, pepper and garlic powder. Stuff each chop with the cooled filling using toothpicks to secure the opening. Add olive oil to an oven-safe skillet and sear the chops on med-high heat on each side for 1-2 minutes. Cover and bake for about 15 minutes, or until the chops are done.

Serve with rice or couscous.

Curried Pork Spareribs

This is a new and improved way to eat spareribs. The warm curry spices and tender veggies in the slow cooker are delicious. Just set it and forget it.

2.5 lbs. pork spareribs
Salt and pepper to taste
1 tablespoon garlic powder
1 teaspoon of each: turmeric and ground coriander
1 tablespoon curry powder
½ yellow onion, thinly sliced
½ cup of canola oil
½ green bell pepper, thinly sliced
1 small carrot, thinly sliced
1 Roma tomato, diced large
2 green onions chopped fine (reserve some for garnish)
1 can of unsweetened coconut milk
½ cup chicken or vegetable stock

Season the spareribs on all sides with salt pepper and garlic powder; set aside. In a small bowl, add the turmeric, ground coriander, curry powder, and olive oil and mix until it turns into a paste. Rub this paste on all sides of the spareribs and place in the slow cooker adding any excess paste to the slow cooker. Add the veggies, coconut milk, and chicken stock. Mix until the veggies are well distributed. Cover and cook on low for 4-6 hours or until the meat is tender and falls off the bone.

Serve with rice.

Chinese 5-Spice Pork Shoulder

The tangy, bold taste of the 5-spice paired with the tender pork shoulder is magical. A great Sunday dinner or anytime you are feeling a little exotic. This makes for a great slow cooker dinner as well.

3 lbs. boneless pork shoulder
2 tablespoons olive oil
Salt and pepper to taste
1 ½ tablespoon Chinese 5 spice
¾ cup of water or beef stock

Preheat oven to 400°F

Drizzle meat with olive oil and season with salt and pepper. Rub the 5-spice onto all sides of the meat. Place in a large roasting dish; cover with aluminum foil and cook for 1 ½ hours or until the meat is tender.

Serve with Jasmine or basmati rice

Cook's note: You can use chuck roast instead of the pork. Just cook for a shorter amount of time. About 45 minutes to 1 hour. Also if you want to use your slow cooker, follow the directions, add meat to your slow cooker and set for 4-6 hours or until tender.

Braised Lamb Chops

For many years now, lamb has been a staple in my family. I'm constantly thinking of different ways to prepare this tasty protein. Slow roasting the lamb gives it the outrageous flavor I'm sure you will enjoy it.

6 blade cut lamb chops
1 large onion, rough chopped
1 small fennel bulb, sliced thick
3 cloves of garlic, peeled and smashed
2 cups of red wine (do not use cooking wine)
2 cups of beef stock
Olive oil
Salt and pepper to taste.

Preheat the oven to 350°F

Salt and pepper the chops; set aside. Meanwhile, preheat a Dutch oven on the stove to medium-high heat and add the chops. Brown on both sides, about 1-2 minutes per side; remove from Dutch oven. Add the onion and fennel and cook for 3-5 minutes or until the veggies are soft. Add the garlic to the onion mixture and return the chops to the Dutch oven. Add the red wine and beef stock; cover and place in the oven for 1½ hours.

Serve with brown basmati rice.

Cook's Notes: If you do not want to use red wine, you can either use 2 cups of water or an extra 2 cups of beef broth.

Tisha's
TAKE ON
"Tasty Sides"

Every main dish needs a side dish right? These recipes will satisfy that age old question, "what side dish can I make?" Well don't worry I've got you!

TASTY SIDES

Risotto with Scallops and Peas

Spinach and Sausage Sauté

Southwestern Couscous

Veggie Basmati Rice

Baked Sweet Potato Fries

Spicy Edamame

Quinoa with Roasted Red Pepper and Pine Nuts

Cold Soba Noodles

Cheesy Cauliflower

Spicy Broccolini

Curried Rice Noodles

Brussels sprouts with Crispy Pancetta

Orzo with Lemon and Basil

Parmesan Couscous

Jasmine Rice Pilaf

Pineapple/Coconut Slaw

Baked Zucchini

Risotto with Scallops & Peas

There are so many different ways to prepare risotto, but I've never seen a scallop and pea combination. The delicate taste of the scallops and the sweetness of the peas turned out to be a great addition to this rice dish.

2 cups of Arborio rice
3 tablespoons of olive oil, divided
4-5 cups of chicken stock (see Cook's notes)
1 cup of frozen peas
1 pound of sea scallops (the large ones)
1 cup Parmesan cheese (see Cook's notes)
Salt & pepper to taste
¼ cup of chopped dill

In a large skillet, add 1 tablespoon of olive oil and sear scallops for about 1 minute per side, remove and set aside; add the peas to the same skillet and cook for 1-2 minutes or until peas are warm and set aside. Place chicken stock in a pot and bring to a simmer (stock must stay warm to make the risotto). In another large pot, add the remaining olive oil and rice; sauté until the rice is light brown. Begin to add the warm chicken stock to the rice one cup at a time until the rice has absorbed the stock. Repeat this process until the rice is creamy (not watery). Salt and pepper to taste. Gently stir in the cheese & peas, place seared scallops on top and garnish with dill.

Serve warm.

Cook's Notes: You may or may not use all of your chicken stock. Also because the Parmesan cheese is salty, you may or may not have to use salt.

Spinach & Sausage Sauté

I love spinach. It's good for your body and incredibly easy to prepare. I'm always looking for new things to do with this versatile vegetable. Here, I've added pre-cooked chicken sausage in this tasty sauté.

6 pre-cooked chicken sausage, cut into coins
16 oz of curly spinach, cleaned and roughly chopped
½ small onion, sliced thin

2 garlic cloves, sliced
2-3 tablespoons olive oil
Salt and pepper to taste
½ teaspoon red pepper flakes

To a large skillet, add olive oil, onion and sausage coins; cook for about 5 minutes or until the sausage is warmed through. Add the spinach and garlic and continue to cook until spinach has wilted down by half. Season with salt, pepper, and red pepper flakes.

Serve warm.

Cook's note: If you cannot find curly spinach, just use regular spinach.

Southwestern Couscous

My mother fed us kids' couscous back when couscous was not as common. We didn't always like it, but we ate it. As I grew up I discovered that I can make my own creations using this tiny pasta. Use it as a side or a meal in itself.

One package of plain couscous
1 teaspoon lime zest
The juice of ½ of a lime
1 clove garlic, minced
1 tablespoon New Mexican Chili Powder
½ cup black beans, drained
½ cup canned corn, drained
½ cup red bell pepper, diced fine
1/3 cup cilantro, chopped fine

Prepare couscous as directed on the package. To the warm couscous, add the lime zest, lime juice, garlic, and chili powder. Mix together with a fork (not a spoon, you will smash the couscous). Mix in black beans, corn, bell pepper, and cilantro.

Serve at room temperature.

Cook's Notes: Treat this like a pasta salad. Add your favorite flavors and create your own tasty combinations.

Veggie Basmati Rice

In need of a side dish to go with my entrée, I began to raid my fridge to see what I can come up with. I like this dish, it's simple and you get your veggies and rice all at the same time.

1 cup of brown basmati rice
¼ teaspoon cumin seeds, toasted
1 cup of frozen mixed veggies
1 ¾ cups of water or vegetable stock
Lemon pepper to taste

Preheat oven to 400°F

Rinse rice under cold water for 30 seconds. Drain and add the rice to an ovenproof skillet. Dry cook the rice until it smells nutty. Add toasted cumin seeds, mixed veggies, and stock. Bring to a boil. Cover and place in the oven for 35 minutes or until the liquid evaporates. Add lemon pepper to taste. Fluff with a fork and serve.

Cook's Notes: You can add toasted pine nuts for an extra crunch.

Baked Sweet Potato Fries

This is a great alternative to regular French fries. They are slightly sweet yet savory, great with hamburgers or fish.

1- 2 large sweet potatoes
Olive oil
Salt and pepper to taste
1 teaspoon sugar

Preheat oven to 450°F

Clean and peel potatoes. Cut in half lengthwise, then cut each half into wedges. Transfer to a bowl and add the olive oil, salt, pepper, and sugar. Mix until each potato is well coated. Move to a parchment-lined cookie sheet. Bake for 25-35 minutes.

Spicy Edamame

This is a very healthy dish. You can use it as a tasty side or as a meal in itself. Full of protein and spicy goodness.

1-2 tablespoons of olive oil
16 oz frozen edamame, shelled
½ small onion, sliced thin
1 clove garlic, sliced
1 red bell pepper, sliced into thin sticks
Salt and pepper to taste
1 ½ teaspoon of red pepper flakes
1/3 – ½ cup of water (if needed)

To a large skillet, add olive oil, edamame, and onion; cook for 2-3 minutes. Add garlic, red bell pepper, red pepper flake, and salt and pepper to taste. Continue to cook for another 5-8 minutes or until vegetables are tender. Only add the water if the pan seems too dry.

Serve warm.

Cook's Notes: More add-ins: cooked pancetta pieces of cooked turkey bacon.

Quinoa with Roasted Peppers and Pine Nuts

I discovered this grain years ago in college, it's so versatile! I sometimes make a meal out of this and have it for dinner instead of meat. I get the protein I need and I feel satisfied.

1 cup uncooked quinoa
2 cups chicken stock
¾ cup red bell peppers, chopped
2 scallions, chopped fine
½ cup toasted pine nuts
Salt and pepper to taste
Olive oil

In a saucepan, combine the quinoa and chicken stock. Cover with a lid, bring to a boil and cook for about 10-15 minutes or until the liquid has evaporated. Add salt and pepper and fluff with a fork. Add the chopped roasted red bell peppers, scallion, and the toasted pine nuts. Transfer to a serving bowl, drizzle with olive oil and enjoy.

Cook's Notes: Quinoa is a really good source of protein and is gluten-free. You can treat this like rice or pasta and add your favorite items to the mix.

Cold Soba Noodle Salad

Fresh, easy, tasty and healthy; what more can you ask for in this cold salad? It is very versatile so be creative and add your favorite mix-ins.

½ lbs. soba noodles
½ cup radicchio, shredded
½ cup fresh zucchini, medium diced
8 crimini (baby Bella) mushrooms, cut into quarters
1 small shallot, minced
Salt and pepper to taste
¼ cup olive oil
¼ cup Balsamic vinegar

Cook the soba noodles according to package directions, drain and set aside. In a medium skillet, add enough olive oil to coat the bottom of the skillet and add the radicchio, zucchini, mushroom, shallots salt and pepper; cook on medium-high heat for about 5 minutes or until the veggies are warmed through. Add mixture to the soba noodles and drizzle the olive oil and balsamic vinegar on top; mix until well incorporated, adding more salt and pepper if needed. Chill in the fridge for about 30 minutes and enjoy.

Cook's Notes: Garnish with sliced scallions & black sesame seeds.

Cheesy Cauliflower

Cauliflower can be a little boring; my cheesy offering will have your family asking for a second helping.

1 head of cauliflower
Salt and pepper to taste
Olive oil
3 tablespoons of butter
3 tablespoons of all-purpose flour
2 cups evaporated milk
3 cups cheddar cheese, shredded
1 cup toasted panko crumbs (see below for instructions)

Preheat oven to 375°F

For the cauliflower: Break into individual florets and add to a large pot of salted boiling water and cook for about 5 minutes (this method is called blanching). Drain, add olive oil and salt and pepper to taste; set aside.

For the cheese sauce: Add butter and flour to a medium skillet and mix with a whisk until smooth; cook for about 3 minutes. Slowly whisk in the milk, salt, and pepper. Continue to whisk until the mixture becomes thick. Turn off the heat and with a wooden spoon, stir in the cheese until completely melted and smooth.

For the toasted panko: Add panko bread crumbs to a dry skillet and cook on medium heat until golden brown.

Spray a casserole dish with non-stick spray and add the cauliflower to the dish. Pour the cheese sauce on top. Top with panko crumbs and bake for 30 minutes or until hot and bubbly.

Cook's Notes: You can also use Swiss cheese or spicy chipotle cheddar to replace the regular cheddar.

Spicy Broccolini

This is such a tasty side. If you love broccoli, you will love this spicy dish.

1 ½ lb. Broccolini
Olive oil
1 teaspoon salt
½ teaspoon of pepper
1 tablespoon of red pepper flakes
2 cloves garlic, sliced
1/3 cup of water

In a large skillet, heat on medium-high and add the olive oil and the Broccolini; cook for about 3 minutes or until the vegetable turns a vibrant green. Add the garlic, salt, pepper, and red pepper flakes; stir until seasoning is well distributed. Add the water, cover and cook for an additional 5 minutes or until tender, but not mushy.

Curried Rice Noodles

These noodles are so tasty. You'll enjoy the smoky flavor of the curry and the fresh taste of the vegetables. Great all by itself or as a side dish.

1 pkg. rice noodles
4 cups of boiling hot water
1 small red bell pepper, cut into thin strips
1 large zucchini, cut into thin strips
1 small onion, thinly sliced
1 garlic clove, minced
Olive oil
Salt and pepper
½ cup vegetable stock
1 teaspoon sesame oil
1 teaspoon turmeric powder
1 heaping tablespoon of yellow curry powder
¼ teaspoon of ground cumin
½ teaspoon of red pepper flakes

For the noodles: In a bowl, add the boiling water to the rice noodles; set aside for 10 minutes or until noodles are soft. Drain and return to the bowl. To a large skillet, add the olive oil, onion, red bell pepper zucchini, and garlic – salt and pepper to taste. Sauté for 8-10 minutes or until the vegetables are slightly brown and soft. Combine the vegetable mixture and the drained noodles together and set aside.

For the sauce: In a small bowl, combine the vegetable stock, sesame oil, turmeric, curry powder, cumin and red pepper flakes; whisk until well incorporated. Pour over the rice & vegetable mixture – mix until the sauce is well incorporated and has coated the noodles and vegetables.

Cook's Note: Add-ins for this dish: cooked chicken or shrimp.

Brussels sprouts with Crispy Pancetta

Brussels sprouts have most certainly gotten a bad rap in the vegetable world. Roasting this tiny green veggie will give it a depth of flavor, and combining it with the savory pancetta will add the salty balance this yummy veggie needs. Not only is it flavorful, but it's also a very unique way to enjoy this tasty vegetable.

1 lb. fresh Brussels sprouts, cleaned and halved
½ cup pancetta, cubed
Pepper
Salt (optional)
Olive oil
1/3 cup water

Coat the bottom of a large skillet with olive oil; add the pancetta and cook for about 3 minutes. Add the Brussels sprouts to the skillet and season with salt and pepper. Continue to cook the sprouts until they start to caramelize. Add the water and cover with a lid for 5 minutes or until the vegetable is tender.

Cook's Note: Pancetta is salty, so go easy on the salt in this dish. Also, if you can't find pancetta in your area, you can follow this same recipe just utilize bacon instead of the pancetta.

Orzo with Lemon and Basil

This is a great pasta to play around with. It's small like a grain of rice and works with a wide variety of ingredients.

1 lb. orzo
½ cup fresh basil, chopped
2 tbs. olive oil
Salt and pepper to taste
Zest of one lemon
Juice of one lemon

Cook the orzo according to box directions and drain; salt and pepper to taste. Add the olive oil, lemon zest and the lemon juice; mix well. Stir in the chopped basil and serve.

Parmesan Couscous

Couscous is very versatile. In this recipe, I use tasty Parmesan cheese and Italian parsley to give this couscous great flavor.

1 cup plain uncooked couscous
1 ½ cups chicken stock
¼ cup Italian parsley, chopped fine
½ cup Parmesan cheese, grated fine
Salt and pepper to taste
Olive oil

In a medium pot, bring the chicken stock to a rolling boil; reduce the heat to medium heat. In a medium bowl, add the uncooked couscous. Slowly add the chicken stock, cover with plastic wrap and set aside for about 5 minutes.

Uncover the couscous and add the salt, pepper, parsley, and Parmesan cheese; gently fluff until the ingredients are well incorporated. Drizzle with olive oil and serve.

Cook's notes: Great with chicken, fish or pork.

Jasmine Rice Pilaf

Jasmine rice is so fragrant. Toasting it gives it even more flavor. You will enjoy this really easy pilaf. You'll never buy boxed again.

1 cup of jasmine rice
1 cup of chicken stock
1 cup of water
1 tablespoon of butter
1 tablespoon of olive oil
¼ cup Italian parsley, chopped
1 small shallot, chopped
1 clove garlic, chopped
Salt and pepper to taste
Juice of ½ lemons

In a skillet, add the olive oil, butter, shallot, and garlic. Cook for about 2 -3 minutes. Add the rice and sauté for about 3-5 minutes. Add the parsley, chicken stock, and water and stir until well combined. Bring to a boil then reduce the heat to low; cover and cook for about 15-18 or until the liquid has evaporated. Add the lemon juice, salt, and pepper. Fluff with a fork and serve.

Pineapple/Coconut Slaw

Y ou will enjoy this fresh, unique slaw. It's good as a side dish or as a light lunch.

4 cups fresh pineapple, medium diced
2 cups of shredded coconut
½ cup golden raisins
Salt and pepper to taste
½ cup chopped walnuts, toasted
¾ cup sour cream
2 tablespoons plain yogurt
1 teaspoon of honey
½ teaspoon fresh jalapeño pepper, seeded and diced fine
1 teaspoon cilantro, chopped fine
Juice of one lemon

In a large bowl, add the pineapple, coconut, raisins, walnuts and the salt and pepper to taste; mix until well combined. In a separate bowl, combine the sour cream, yogurt, jalapeño, cilantro, and lemon juice; mix until all ingredients are well incorporated. Fold in the pineapple mixture. Stash in the fridge for at least an hour, but two would be better.

Cook's Notes: If you want to add more kick to this dish, leave the seeds in the jalapeño.

Baked Zucchini

Back in the day, I certainly did not care for zucchini, but now I've got a new appreciation for this delicious vegetable. I've updated some ingredients to give a more gourmet swag.

4 large zucchini, cut into large rounds
1 cup of fresh bread crumbs
½ cup Italian parsley, minced
½ cup Romano cheese
1 small shallot, minced
Salt and pepper to taste
Olive oil
Zest of one lemon

Preheat oven to 400°F

Place the zucchini rounds in a casserole dish, add salt and pepper and drizzle with olive oil; set aside. In a skillet, drizzle olive oil and add the breadcrumbs, shallot, and parsley; cook for about 2 or 3 minutes until warmed through. Pour the bread crumb mixture over top of the zucchini, spreading it out evenly. Add the lemon zest on top and bake for about 20-25 minutes or until the zucchini is tender and the bread crumbs are brown.

Tisha's
TAKE ON
"Vegetarian Options"

It's okay to lay off meat from time to time. These recipes are tasty and will satisfy every meat lover you know. You won't miss that meat or chicken.

VEGETARIAN OPTIONS

Roasted Eggplant Lasagna

Veggie Sauté with Garlic Fettuccine

Grilled Veggies on Sourdough

Chickpea Salad

Curry Cauliflower

Portobello Burger

Panko Crusted Tofu with Sriracha Cream Sauce

Portobello /Caramelized Onion French Breaded Pizza

Tomato and Brie Panini

Quinoa Fritter Sandwich

Butternut and Chickpea Sauté

Wild Mushrooms with White Bean and Spinach

Gnocchi with Escarole and Yellow Squash

Fried Egg over Chips

Roasted Eggplant Lasagna

A tasty alternative to traditional lasagna and you get your veggies in too. Vegetarians and meat-eaters alike will enjoy this hardy dish.

2 medium eggplants, cubed
1 medium onion, diced
2 cloves garlic, minced
Salt and pepper to taste
3 tablespoons olive oil, divided
26 oz pasta sauce
4 basil leaves chopped
1 cup pesto, divided
10 oz ricotta cheese
16 oz shredded mozzarella cheese (save 2 cups)
6-8 lasagna noodles

Preheat oven to 400°F

To the cubed eggplant, add salt, pepper and 1 tablespoon olive oil. Toss to coat and transfer to a baking sheet. Bake for 30-40 minutes and set aside. In a large skillet, add the remaining olive oil and onion and cook for about 5 minutes or until the onions are soft. To the skillet, add the eggplant, garlic, pasta sauce, and basil; simmer for about 10-15 minutes. While the mixture is simmering, in a small bowl, mix together the ricotta, mozzarella, and egg; set aside. In a glass casserole dish, lay down 4 of the uncooked lasagna noodles. Spread some of the eggplant mixture on the noodles, then spread on some of the cheese mixture and half of the pesto. Repeat this process for the remaining ingredients. Top with the remainder of the eggplant mixture and the two cups of mozzarella cheese. Reduce the oven to 375°F and bake for 45-55 minutes or until hot and bubbly.

Veggie Sauté with Garlic Fettuccine

In this dish, you'll get to adventure with the freshness of the sautéed veggies the spicy kick of the pasta. Who said going vegetarian has to be boring?

2 cups fresh broccoli florets
2 cups asparagus, cut into 1-inch pieces
1 ½ cup grape tomatoes
2 cloves garlic, sliced
Salt and pepper to taste
1 teaspoon red pepper flakes
1 tablespoon olive oil
½ cup water or vegetable stock
1 pound fettuccine
Salt and pepper to taste
3 garlic cloves, minced
2 tablespoons butter

In a large deep-sided skillet, add the olive oil, broccoli, and asparagus. Cook for about two minutes or until the vegetables turn a vibrant green. Add the garlic, salt, and pepper and continue to cook for another 3 minutes. Add the tomatoes, red pepper flake and water to the skillet. Cover the skillet and turn the heat to low and simmer for 5 minutes. Serve with the garlic fettuccine.

For the garlic fettuccine: Cook the pasta according to the box directions. Drain and add the minced garlic, butter, and salt and pepper to taste. Mix until the butter is melted.

Grilled Veggies on Sourdough

This is a great any time meal. The grilled veggies give this sandwich a smoky flavor. The vinaigrette gives a little tang to the whole dish.

1 eggplant, sliced lengthwise (see cook's note)
1 medium red onion, cut into 1-inch slices
1 large red bell pepper, cut into quarters
2 medium zucchini, sliced lengthwise
6 asparagus
8 basil leaves
Salt and pepper
1/3 cup olive oil (plus 2 tablespoons)
1 large sourdough round, sliced in half horizontally
½ cup of red wine vinaigrette

In a large bowl, add all of the veggies, 1/3 cup olive oil, salt, and pepper; toss to make sure all the veggies are well coated. Grill until the veggies are tender, about 15-20 minutes. Set aside to cool.

To assemble the sandwich: Remove some of the bread from each half of the sourdough. Brush the sourdough halves with the remaining olive oil. In single layers, add the eggplant, onion, red bell pepper, zucchini, and asparagus. Top with the basil leaves and drizzle the vinaigrette over the top. Tightly wrap the whole thing in plastic wrap and set in the fridge for one hour. Slice into wedges and serve.

Cook's note: before cooking or seasoning, add a little bit of salt to both side of the eggplant and place on a rack over the sink for about 30 minutes. Rinse the salt off and dry completely before using it. You'll notice the eggplant will be very pliable and not stiff. Much easier to work within this recipe.

Chickpea Salad

I love this salad because it is so versatile and refreshing. The ingredients on the list are just my favs; get creative and add your own twist.

One 19oz can of chickpeas, drained
½ of an English cucumber, diced
1 cup grape tomatoes, cut in half
½ cup of reduced-fat feta cheese
1 ½ cup of asparagus, cut into ½ inch pieces
½ of a medium zucchini, diced
½ of medium red bell pepper, diced
½ cup flat-leaf parsley, finely chopped
1 teaspoon lemon pepper
½ cup balsamic vinaigrette dressing

Bring a large pot of water to a simmer. Add the asparagus, zucchini, and red bell pepper to the simmering water for about 2-3 minutes, 'blanching' the vegetables. Remove from the water and immediately rinse with cold water. In a large bowl, add the chickpeas, cucumber, grape tomatoes, the blanched vegetables, feta cheese, parsley, lemon pepper, and the dressing. Stir until all ingredients are mixed together. Chill for at least 1 hour, but overnight would be better.

Serve with sourdough or pita bread.

Curry Cauliflower

This vegetable is very versatile. In this recipe, vegetarians and meat-eaters alike will enjoy the smoky, spicy flavors this curry dish offers.

1 head of cauliflower
Salt and pepper to taste
1 tablespoon olive oil
1 small onion, diced
2 cloves garlic, minced
1 red bell pepper, sliced into sticks
18 oz. jar of red curry sauce
1 tablespoon smooth peanut butter
1 cup chicken stock

Cut the head of cauliflower into individual florets. To a large preheated skillet, add the olive oil, and onion; cook for about 2-3 minutes or until the onions are soft. Add the cauliflower florets, red bell pepper, garlic, salt, and pepper. Cook for another 2 minutes. Add the red curry sauce, peanut butter, and chicken stock. Mix until the sauce is smooth. Simmer for 10-15 minutes or until the cauliflower is tender.

Serve with rice.

Portobello Burger

This great meat substitute. Portobello mushrooms are very meaty and the flavor is enhanced by putting them on the grill or broiling them.

4 Portobello mushroom caps
4 slices pepper jack cheese
4 Potato rolls

For the Marinade:
1 cup olive oil
1 teaspoon each salt and pepper
2 garlic cloves, minced
½ teaspoon liquid smoke
1 teaspoon red pepper flakes
4-6 dashes Worcestershire sauce

In a large zip-top bag, combine all of the marinade ingredients. Whisk to make sure everything is well incorporated. Add the Portobello caps; make sure the marinade touches every part of the mushrooms. Set in the fridge for about 30 minutes. Remove any excess marinade and grill for about 5 minutes per side. Add the cheese for the last 5 minutes. Serve on toasted hamburger buns.

Cook's note: Don't want to grill? You can also broil these in your oven.

Panko Crusted Tofu with Sriracha Cream Sauce

Now, I understand that some people may be turned off by the thought of eating tofu, but I challenge you to give my recipe a try. It's crunchy, full of flavor and you won't miss the meat at all. It will make you a believer.

8 oz. firm tofu
½ cup low sodium soy sauce
2 tablespoons rice vinegar
1 teaspoon sesame oil
¼ teaspoon red pepper flakes (optional)
½ teaspoon grated ginger

½ cup flour
1 egg, slightly beaten
1 ½ cup panko bread crumbs
Canola oil
Sriracha cream sauce (see below)

Drain the tofu and pat dry. Cut the tofu into cubes and set aside. In a small bowl, whisk together the soy sauce, vinegar, sesame oil, red pepper flakes, and grated ginger until well incorporated. Add the tofu cubes to the mixture; coat all sides, cover and let it marinate for at least 2 hours (overnight would be better). Drain the tofu and pat dry. Coat the cubes with flour, dip in the egg and coat with the panko bread crumbs – shake off the excess and fry until golden brown.

Sriracha Cream Sauce:

6 oz plain Greek yogurt
1 garlic clove, minced fine
1/3 cup Sriracha hot sauce (add more if you dare)

Whisk all of the ingredients together until well incorporated. Serve on top or on the side for dipping.

Cook's note: Garnish with slivered almonds and chopped scallions.

Portobello & Caramelized Onion French Breaded Pizza

I remember eating French breaded pizza at home and in elementary school. It was quick and easy. My family adores mushrooms, so I decided to refresh this old favorite with some upgraded ingredients. Hope you enjoy.

1 loaf French bread
1 lb. Portobello mushrooms, slice about ½ inch thick
2-3 Spanish or Vidalia sweet onions, thinly sliced

2 clove garlic
Olive oil
1/3 cup white wine (not cooking wine)
½ cup Italian parsley, chopped
1 teaspoon of red pepper flakes
Salt and pepper
8 oz. marinara sauce, divided
16 oz. provolone cheese, shredded

Preheat oven to 400°F

Cut the French bread loaf in half lengthwise and remove some of the bread on the inside. Brush halves with olive oil, season with salt and pepper and place on a baking sheet; set aside.

In a large hot skillet, add the olive oil and mushrooms. Cook the mushrooms for a few minutes then add the garlic, white wine, and red pepper flakes; salt and pepper to taste. Cook until the white wine has been absorbed and the pan is dry; mix in the parsley and set aside.

Caramelized onion: Add the thinly sliced onion to a skillet along with a tablespoon of olive oil. Cook until the onions have reduced by half and have turned a yummy golden brown color (this process will take 15-20 mins). Set aside.

To assemble: To one half of the French bread, add 4 oz of marinara sauce, half of the mushroom mixture and top with half of the provolone cheese. Repeat this process with the second half of bread. Bake for about 10-15 minutes or until the cheese has melted and the bread is toasted.

Cooke's note: You can substitute the provolone cheese with smoked mozzarella which is also very tasty.

Tomato and Brie Panini

I love the combination of the tender tomato, the tangy brie and sweet onions on the chewy ciabatta bread. Strange combo I know, but your taste buds will be happy.

6 slices of brie cheese
6 slices of tomato
Olive oil
1 cup caramelized onion, divided (recipe follows)
5 oz baby spinach, divided
3 ciabatta rolls, sliced lengthwise
Salt and pepper

Preheat your Panini Press.

Take each roll and brush all sides with olive oil.

Caramelized onion: add the thinly sliced onion to a skillet along with a tablespoon of olive oil. Cook until the onions have reduced by half and have turned a yummy golden brown color (this process will take 15-20 min). Set aside.

To assemble panini: Take half of one roll and place some baby spinach, caramelized onion and two slices of tomato; season with salt and pepper. Top with two slices of brie and place on the Panini. Repeat the process with the remaining ingredients.

Place each one into your Panini press and cook for about 3-5 minutes or until flat and melty. Slice in half and serve with fries or a salad.

Cooke's note: If you do not have a Panini press, not to worry, you can use something like a George Foreman grill. You can also substitute the brie with fontina or Gruyere cheese.

Quinoa Fritter Sandwich

This is similar to falafel, except quinoa is packed with protein. So even though this lightly fried, it is still relatively healthy for you.

2 cups cooked quinoa
½ cup green onion, chopped fine
1 clove garlic, finely minced
¼ cup zucchini, grated
¼ cup roasted red pepper, chopped fine
Salt and pepper to taste
¼ teaspoon red pepper flakes (optional)
½ teaspoon ground cumin
1 tablespoon flour
½ cup panko bread crumbs
1 egg

In a large bowl, combine the quinoa, garlic, zucchini, roasted bell pepper, salt, pepper, red pepper flakes, and cumin. Mix until well incorporated. Stir in the olive oil, flour, egg, and panko crumbs; set in the fridge for about 30 minutes. Form into medium-sized patties, and lightly fry on each side for about 3 minutes per side or until brown and crispy. Drain excess oil.

Cook's Note: Serve in pita bread with lettuce, tomato, and roasted red pepper aioli.

Butternut and Chickpea Sauté

I am constantly thinking of different ways to go vegetarian. The combination of the chickpea, squash and sweet coconut milk will take your taste buds on an exotic journey your waistline will appreciate.

12 oz butternut squash, cubed
8 oz canned chickpea, drained
½ onion, diced
2 garlic cloves, diced
Olive oil
¼ cup Italian parsley, chopped
Salt and pepper to taste
¼ teaspoon each: ground cumin, ground ginger, and nutmeg
1 teaspoon curry powder
½ cup vegetable stock
½ cup light coconut milk

In a large skillet, coat bottom with olive oil and add the onion, garlic and butternut squash. Cook for about 5 minutes and then add the chickpeas. Season with salt and pepper, add all of the spices and vegetable stock; mix well and simmer on low until the butternut squash is tender. Stir in the coconut milk and simmer for 5 more minutes. Top with chopped parsley.

Cook's note: Serve with brown basmati or jasmine rice.

Wild Mushrooms with White Beans and Spinach

This dish was inspired by a friend of mine who is a vegetarian and absolutely loves mushrooms. This is a very satisfying dish even for meat-eaters.

4 oz Crimini mushrooms (Baby Bellas)
4 oz Portobello mushrooms
4 oz shitake mushrooms
4 oz oyster mushrooms
1 large shallot, minced
Olive oil to coat the pan
¼ cup white dry wine
Salt and pepper to taste
1 teaspoon ground cumin
10 oz curly spinach, cleaned and roughly chopped
1 - 15oz can of cannellini beans, drained
Chopped Italian parsley and Parmesan cheese for garnish

Rough chop all of the mushrooms and add them along with the shallot to a large skillet coated with olive oil; salt and pepper to taste. Cook until the mushrooms are soft. Add the beans and cumin, and simmer for about 5-10 minutes. Finally, add the spinach and cook until the spinach has wilted down. Top with chopped Italian parsley and Parmesan cheese.

Cook's note: You can use kale instead of spinach.

Gnocchi with Escarole and Yellow Squash

I am always looking to create healthy, satisfying dishes for some of my vegetarian friends. Who wants to eat pasta primavera all the time? This dish will always hit the spot.

1 lb. of gnocchi
1 lb. of escarole
2 large yellow squash, large diced

Olive oil
Salt and pepper to taste
Pecorino cheese

Cook the gnocchi according to package directions (or if you are ambitious, you can make your own). In a large skillet, add the olive oil, squash and salt, and pepper; cook until the squash is fork-tender. Add the escarole and more salt and pepper if needed. Cook for an additional 5 minutes or until the escarole has wilted. Drain the gnocchi and add to the squash mixture. Mix well, top with cheese, and serve.

Fried Egg and Chips

I am very fortunate to have friends from literally all over the globe. I love the fact that I can not only enjoy these different cuisines, but I can also put my own creative spin on the dish. This dish was inspired by a friend of mine who is from the UK. It's crispy and creamy all at the same time. Who would guess something so simple could taste so good?

2 large russet potatoes (these will
be the 'chips')
4 extra-large eggs
Salt and pepper
Canola oil for frying
Non-stick spray
Chopped Italian parsley

Clean potatoes (skin on) and cut each potato into thick strips. Fry in about 1 inch of oil for about 10 minutes or until brown and crispy. Drain and season with salt and pepper while still hot. In a clean skillet, spray with non-stick spray and crack the eggs two at a time, careful not to break the yolk. Fry for about 1 ½ minutes on one side then carefully flip and cook on the second side for about 10 to 15 seconds. Repeat this for the other two eggs (the yolk should be runny). Place fries on two individual plates and place 2 eggs on top of one plate of chips; repeat for the second plate.

Cook's note: Garnish with parsley.

Tisha's
TAKE ON
"Simple Sauces and Dressings"

These sauces are just what the titles says. Simple. Sauces are
a great addition to some of the recipes in this book.

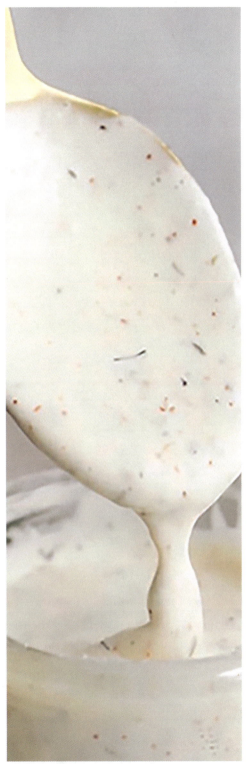

SIMPLE SAUCES AND DRESSINGS

Curry Aioli

Garlic Aioli

Chipotle Sauce

Sweet and Spicy Sauce

Peanut Sauce

Wasabi Tartar Sauce

Mustard Sauce

Roasted Red Pepper Cream Sauce

Citrus Vinaigrette

Pomegranate Vinaigrette

Lemony Lemon Vinaigrette

Salsa Verde

Curry Aioli

1 tablespoon mayonnaise
3 oz sour cream or plain Greek yogurt
1 garlic clove
1 teaspoon curry powder
Pinch of ground cumin
1 teaspoon fresh lemon juice

Combine all ingredients in a food processor or blender and serve.

Garlic Aioli

1 tablespoon mayonnaise
3 oz sour cream or plain Greek yogurt
1 garlic clove
1 teaspoon fresh lemon juice

Combine all ingredients in a food processor or blender and serve. Try and make this ahead, as the garlic will have time to penetrate the mayo and sour cream/yogurt.

Chipotle Sauce

1-2 Adobo chipotle peppers (3 if you want an extra kick)
1 garlic clove
6 oz low-fat plain yogurt
3 oz low-fat sour cream
Salt and pepper to taste (if needed)
1-2 tablespoons chicken stock (as needed to thin the sauce)

Add all ingredients to a blender or food processor. Mix until all ingredients are well incorporated and smooth. Check for seasoning and salt and pepper to taste if needed.

Sweet and Spicy Sauce

1 heaping tablespoon garlic chili paste
½ cup chutney
¼ cup chicken stock
1 teaspoon low-sodium soy sauce
1 teaspoon honey

Combine all ingredients in a saucepan until well incorporated and warmed throughout, about 3-5 minutes.

Peanut Sauce

1 cup smooth peanut butter
4 tablespoons tahini paste (sesame paste)
2 tablespoons low-fat plain yogurt
2 tablespoons low-sodium soy sauce
1 garlic clove
1 teaspoon fresh ginger
½ - ¾ cup warm chicken broth

In a food processor or blender, combine all ingredients until smooth. Add more chicken stock if needed to thin out the sauce.

Wasabi Tartar Sauce

2 heaping tablespoons of mayonnaise
1 tablespoon sweet pickle relish
½ teaspoon Wasabi paste
¼ teaspoon white pepper
Dash of lime juice

Mix all the ingredients together and stash in the refrigerator for at least 2 hours. Overnight would be better.

Mustard Sauce

4 pats butter, divided
¼ cup olive oil
2 garlic cloves, minced
2 tablespoons balsamic vinegar
3 heaping tablespoons stone-ground mustard
¼ - 1/3 cup chicken stock (or water)
1 tablespoon low-fat sour cream
½ cup Italian parsley

In a non-stick skillet, add 2 pats of butter, olive oil, and garlic. Cook for about 2 minutes. Add the vinegar, mustard, and chicken stock and mix until smooth. Finally, add the remaining butter pats, sour cream, and parsley.

Roasted Red Pepper Cream Sauce

One 8 oz jar roasted red bell peppers
1 garlic clove
Salt and pepper to taste
1 tablespoon Italian Parsley
8 oz plain Greek yogurt
1 or 2 tablespoons warm chicken or vegetable stock

Add all of the ingredients (except the vegetable stock) into a food processor and blend until smooth. Slowly drizzle the chicken or vegetable stock until the mixture is the consistency you like.

Citrus Vinaigrette

½ cup of orange juice
Zest of one orange
Salt and pepper to taste
2 tablespoons peach balsamic vinegar
½ shallot, finely minced
1 cup olive oil

Add all ingredients to a medium-sized jar and shake until well incorporated.

Pomegranate Vinaigrette

½ cup pomegranate juice
Zest and juice from one lemon
Salt and pepper to taste
¾ cup olive oil

Add all ingredients to a medium-sized jar and shake until well incorporated.

Lemony Lemon Vinaigrette

½ cup fresh lemon juice
1 garlic clove, minced
1 teaspoon Dijon mustard
Zest from one lemon
Salt and pepper to taste
¾ cup olive oil

Add all ingredients to a medium sized jar and shake until well incorporated.

Salsa Verde

6 tomatillos, quartered
2 to 3 Jalapeños
3 garlic cloves
1 small onion, quartered
¼ cup vegetable stock
Salt and pepper to taste
Olive oil

Preheat oven to 400°F

Place the tomatillos, garlic cloves and the onion to the sheet pan. Drizzle with olive oil and season with salt and pepper. Roast for about 30 minutes or until soft. Set aside to cool for about 10 minutes, and then add the mixture to a food processor, drizzle the vegetable stock until the salsa is the consistency you like.

Tisha's
TAKE ON
"Sweet Stuff"

Who doesn't end a great dinner with yummy dessert? These recipes are decadent, delicious and pretty easy to prepare. Guaranteed to satisfy your sweet tooth.

SWEET STUFF

Sweet Banana Egg Roll with Vanilla Ice Cream

Chocolate Raspberry Torte

Banana Cake with Vanilla Bean Butter Cream

Chocolate Chip Cream Cheese Bars

Easy Coconut Brittle

Cinnamon Sugar Crisp

Piña Colada Cream Pie

Baked Pineapple

Individual Blackberry Trifles

Pineapple Cranberry Bread Pudding

Sweet Banana Egg Roll with Mango Ice Cream

This dessert is crispy, sinful, decadent... it's just downright delicious.

2 cardamom seeds, crushed
½ cup dark brown sugar
¼ teaspoon allspice
1 teaspoon vanilla
2 tablespoons dark rum
1 tablespoon water
3 large ripe banana, medium diced
1 tablespoon lemon zest
Large wonton wrappers
Oil for frying
Mango ice cream

Add the crushed cardamom seeds to a large, dry, non-stick skillet and cook for about 2 minutes. Add the brown sugar, allspice, vanilla, and water; cook until the sugar has melted. Add the diced banana, lemon zest, and rum; cook until the banana is warmed through and the sauce is thick. Set aside and cool down completely. Don't forget to remove the cardamom seeds.

To assemble the egg roll: Take one wonton wrapper and place 2 tablespoons of the banana mixture onto the wrapper. Begin to roll once then fold the edges inward – continue to gently roll until you come to the end. Repeat the process until the mixture and/or the wrappers are gone. Seam side down, place the filled rolls onto the skillet with at least 1 inch of oil. Fry on each side until golden brown. Remove from oil and drain. Cool for about 10 minutes and dust with confectioners' sugar. Serve with mango ice cream.

Chocolate Raspberry Tart

Chocolate and raspberries are simply meant for each other. In this tart, I've added fresh, crushed raspberries to the extra chocolaty dessert. If you love chocolate, then this is the dessert for you.

Tart
1 cup (2 sticks) unsalted butter, cut into pieces
12 oz bittersweet chocolate, chopped
1 teaspoon vanilla
1 ½ cups sugar
6 large eggs, room temperature
2/3 cups flour
¼ teaspoon salt
1 pint fresh raspberries, crushed with 1 teaspoon flour (reserve 3 whole berries for garnish)
1 tablespoon Chambord (raspberry liqueur - optional)
½ cup seedless raspberry jam
A sprig of mint for garnish

Ganache
8 oz semisweet chocolate, chopped
5 oz heavy cream

Preheat oven to 350°F.

For the tart: Spray a 9-inch diameter tart pan with non-stick cooking spray. Melt butter in a large, heavy saucepan over medium heat, stirring until it begins to bubble at the edges. Remove from heat. Add chocolate and let stand for 1 minute. Stir until chocolate is melted and smooth. Add the vanilla, sugar, and eggs, 1 at a time (don't worry if it looks grainy). Add flour and salt; stir gently until all the ingredients are completely incorporated. Fold in raspberries and Chambord and transfer to prepared pan.

Bake tart until the top is puffed, cracked and a tester inserted into the center comes out moist (not wet), about 25-35 minutes. Cool completely in pan on a wire rack. Spread a thin layer of raspberry jam on top of the cooled tart.

For the ganache: In a saucepan, heat heavy cream to a simmer (do not boil). Add chocolate and stir until the chocolate is completely melted and glossy. Pour ganache over the top of the cooled tart and allow it to cool completely.

Banana Cake

This cake is fluffy, moist and chocked full of bananas and walnuts. The addition of rum is an extra kick on the taste buds. Definitely not banana bread, you will be pleasantly surprised.

2 cups flour
2 teaspoons baking powder
1 teaspoon baking soda
½ teaspoon salt

½ cup buttermilk
3 large bananas, smashed
½ cup walnuts (optional)
½ cup of vegetable oil
1 cup of sugar
2 large eggs
1 teaspoon vanilla
2 tablespoons dark rum (optional)

Vanilla Bean Butter Cream:
2 sticks of unsalted butter, softened
3 ½ cups of confectioners' sugar
1 vanilla bean
3 tablespoons of heavy cream

Preheat oven to 350°F

In a medium bowl, mix together the flour, baking powder, baking soda, and salt; set aside. In a medium bowl, stir together the buttermilk, mashed bananas and walnuts. In another bowl, combine the oil, sugar, eggs, and vanilla until light, fluffy and pale. Add the banana mixture to the sugar mixture and mix well. Slowly incorporate the flour mixture until all ingredients are well blended. Mix in the dark rum and pour the batter into an 8-inch non-stick cake pan sprayed with non-stick spray. Bake for 25-30 minutes.

For the vanilla bean buttercream: Add the softened butter and confectioners' sugar to a large bowl and with an electric hand mixer, mix until well incorporated and very fluffy (about 3-5 minutes) Add the seeds of the vanilla bean and the heavy cream. Mix again until well incorporated. Frost or pipe the buttercream onto the cooled cake.

Chocolate Chip Cream Cheese Bars

This dessert is incredibly sinful. I love making these for get-togethers or as gifts. Be ready because this is a very rich, decadent dessert.

2 large pkg chocolate chip cookie dough (I like Nestle)
2 - 8 oz pkg cream cheese, room temperature
1 extra-large egg, slightly beaten
1 teaspoon vanilla
½ teaspoon lemon zest
1 tablespoon lemon juice
1/3 cup sugar
½ cup chopped walnuts (optional)
6 oz bittersweet chocolate (melted for garnish)

Preheat oven to 350°F

In a bowl, combine the softened cream cheese, egg, vanilla, lemon zest, lemon juice, and sugar. With an electric hand mixer, combine ingredients until smooth, about 2 minutes. Set aside.

Press 1 package of chocolate chip cookie dough onto the bottom of the cookie sheet. Spread half of the cream cheese mixture over the cookie dough. Break up the second package of cookie dough into bite-size pieces and dot the top of the cream cheese mixture. Spread the remaining cream cheese mixture over the top of the whole thing. If you opt for the chopped walnuts, sprinkle over top. Bake for 45 - 55 minutes. Use the toothpick test to check for doneness.

Drizzle melted bittersweet chocolate over the top. Cool and cut into squares.

Cook's Notes: If you have the time, you could certainly make the chocolate cookie dough from scratch, which I've done, but using store-bought is perfectly fine. No one will ever know. You can also add a little peanut butter to the cream cheese mixture if you are feeling ambitious.

Easy Coconut Brittle

Making brittle or any type of candy can be very intimidating, but trust me when I say this is the easiest brittle recipe ever with no candy thermometer required. I've made this countless times. The toasted coconut gives it a very unique taste. Great for gifts or just because.

4 cups of sugar
1 cup of water
4 tablespoons butter
2 cups toasted coconut, cooled
Parchment paper

Line a cookie sheet or your counter with a few layers of parchment paper.

In a large heavy saucepan, combine sugar and water. Boil the sugar-water mixture until it becomes a medium amber color; this is the hardball stage in candy making. This process will take 5 - 10 minutes. Don't walk away from the stove. Turn off the heat and quickly stir in the butter and toasted coconut. Transfer the very hot mixture to the countertop or cookie sheet lined with parchment. Spread so the candy is even all around. Allow brittle to cool completely. Gently break the brittle apart and serve.

Cook's Notes: For brittle variation, try adding roughly chopped macadamia nuts, cashews, or Spanish peanuts.

Cinnamon Sugar Crisps

When I was younger, my siblings and I would make these little crisps for a little after school treat. They are inexpensive and easy to make. I've added some ingredients to level up this childhood favorite of mine.

10-12 wonton skins
½ cup of sugar
2 heaping tablespoons cinnamon
½ teaspoon ground ginger
¼ teaspoon nutmeg
Canola oil
Your favorite ice cream (I like raspberry or mango on this dessert)

In a small bowl combine sugar, cinnamon, ginger, and nutmeg and set aside.

In a large skillet, heat canola oil and add 2-3 wonton skins, cooking for about two minutes per side or until light golden brown. Transfer to a wire rack and generously sprinkle the sugar mixture over the hot wonton skins. Repeat this process for the remaining wonton skins. Serve warm with the Mango ice cream.

Piña Colada Cream Pie

This pie was created when my uncle thought it would be a good idea to combine a banana cream pie and a coconut cream pie. I came up with a Piña Colada pie; very tropical, very tasty.

1 - 9-inch pre-made pie shell
5 large egg yolks, slightly beaten
¼ cup cornstarch
¼ cup non-alcoholic piña colada mix
3 cups of milk
¾ cup of sugar
1 cup sweetened coconut flakes
1 teaspoon vanilla
1 tablespoon unsalted butter
2 bananas, diced
 1 cup heavy cream
1/3 cup confectioner's sugar
Toasted coconut for garnish

Preheat oven to 400°F

Blind bake (see cook's notes) the pie crust for about 20 minutes or until golden brown. Set aside to cool.

In a small bowl, mix together egg yolks, cornstarch, and piña colada mix. In a non-stick saucepan, add the milk and sugar. Bring the mixture to just under a boil (scalding). Slowly add ¼ cup of the milk and sugar mixture to the egg mixture 'tempering' the eggs. Slowly whisk the tempered eggs back into the saucepan. Whisk until the mixture has thickened; remove from heat. Add the coconut flakes, vanilla, butter, and diced banana and mix until all the ingredients are well incorporated. Pour the mixture into the cooled prepared pie shell. Cover with plastic wrap and refrigerate for at least 4 hours (overnight would be better). Top with whipped cream and toasted coconut.

For the whipped cream: In a large bowl, add the heavy cream and with an electric mixture, whip until it forms stiff peaks. Sift in the confectioner's sugar and fold into the cream until well combined.

Cook's notes: Blind baking is a process where you bake the pie shell for 15-20 minutes before adding your filling. This prevents crust that is underdone.

Baked Pineapple

Pineapple is great; I love the fresh, sweet taste of this tropical fruit. This is a very unique and tasty way to experience this exotic fruit. You'll appreciate this twist to regular, boring baked pineapple. Enjoy.

1 large ripe pineapple
¾ cup dark brown sugar
1 tablespoon cinnamon

½ teaspoon ground ginger
¼ cup Malibu rum
Vanilla Greek yogurt

Preheat oven to 400°F.

In a bowl, combine the brown sugar, cinnamon, and ginger and rum; set aside. Remove the top, bottom, and skin of the pineapple and cut in half lengthwise. Evenly coat each half of the pineapple with the brown sugar mixture. Transfer to a baking dish and cover with aluminum foil. Bake for 25 minutes or until hot and bubbly. Serve with yogurt.

Cook's Note: You can garnish with toasted pine nuts or toasted pecans.

Individual Blackberry Trifles

Traditionally, this British dessert is served family-style in a trifle container. I thought it would be sexy to break it down and serve this by the glass.

For the Trifle
2 pints of blackberries
1 ½ tablespoon granulated sugar
3 tablespoons blackberry preserves
1 store-bought pound cake
Mint simple syrup (recipe follows)
12 oz heavy whipping cream
1/3 cup confectioners' sugar
Mint leaf for garnish

Mint Simple syrup
½ cup granulated sugar
½ cup of water
2 whole mint leaves

For the mint simple syrup: In a small pot, add the granulated sugar, water, and mint leaves; bring to a boil then reduce the heat to medium for 3-5 minutes or until the sugar is completely dissolved. Remove the mint leaves and set aside to cool completely.

For the trifle: In a glass bowl, add the blackberries and sugar. With a fork, smash the berries and sugar together; mix in the blackberry preserve and set aside. Slice the pound cake into ½ inch slices; line them up and brush each slice with the mint simple syrup. Cut each slice into quarters creating cubes; set aside. Add the heavy whipping cream and confectioners' sugar to a clean bowl, and with an electric hand mixture, begin to whip the heavy cream until it forms stiff peaks. Set aside.

In individual glass parfait cups, begin to layer the ingredients in the following order: 3 cubes of cake, whipped cream then the smashed berry mixture – repeat the process to complete two layers per parfait cup. Stash in the refrigerator for at least an hour. Garnish each with mint leaves.

Pineapple/ Cranberry Bread Pudding

I enjoy traditional bread pudding, but my creative mind could not leave well enough alone. I've road-tested this recipe on a few friends and it's a hit every time.

3 medium croissants, sliced in half and cubed
4 slices of sourdough bread, cubed
1 - 8oz can of crushed pineapple
½ cup of dried cranberries
4 cups of half and half
3 whole large eggs
3 egg yolks
¾ cup of sugar
1 teaspoon vanilla
1 teaspoon lemon zest
1 ½ teaspoon of cinnamon
¼ teaspoon nutmeg
Pinch of kosher salt
Non-stick spray

Preheat oven to 350°F.

Place cubed croissants and sourdough bread on a baking sheet and allow to sit uncovered for about an hour. Meanwhile, in a medium bowl, combine the eggs and sugar together – whisk until well incorporated. Add the half and half, vanilla, lemon zest, cinnamon, nutmeg, and salt – whisk until all ingredients are well incorporated and set aside. Spray a casserole dish with the non-stick spray and place the bread cubes inside. Sprinkle the crushed pineapple (juice and all) evenly over the bread cubes; repeat this process with the dried cranberries.

Pour the egg mixture evenly over the bread and allow resting for about 10 minutes (this will allow the egg mixture to soak into the bread pieces). Place the casserole dish in a water bath (see cook's notes) and bake for 45-60 minutes, depending on your oven.

Serve warm or at room temperature with fresh whipped cream.

Cook's Note: You can substitute raisins for the cranberries and/or half and half with whole milk or heavy cream. To create a water bath, find a container larger than the casserole pan, place the casserole pan inside the larger pan, and then place boiling water into the larger pan – carefully place the whole thing in the oven.

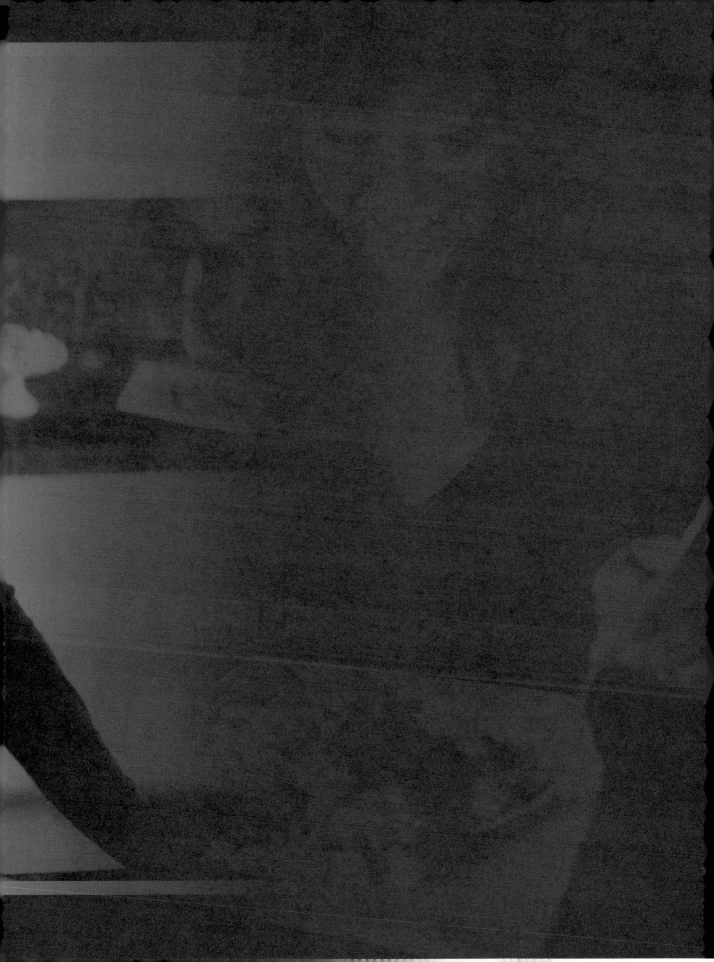

Tisha's
TAKE ON
"Mix it up"

I love a good adult beverage. I felt it was important to add this section
so you can have a complete menu. I was privileged to work with
a good friend of mine on these tasty adult beverages.

MIX IT UP — COCKTAILS AND NON-ALCOHOLIC BEVERAGES

Thai Iced Tea

Iced Chai Tea

Fizzy Pom

Pom Mimosa

Mock Rita

Blue Haze

Purple Passion

Raging Rita

Buttery Scotch

Innocent Envy

Thai Iced Tea

The first time I had this delicious tasty drink I fell in love. I asked the server what was in it; they didn't want to tell me so I immediately tried to figure out myself. Well, I think I did a pretty good job replicating this refreshing drink. I hope you enjoy!

8 cups of water
8 Jasmine black tea bags
½ cup agave syrup (use more if you like it sweeter)
½ inch peeled fresh ginger, sliced

Cardamom seeds & a couple of cinnamon sticks
1 can sweeten condensed milk
Mint leaves for garnish

Bring the water to a boil, turn off the heat and add the tea bags to the pot along with the agave, ginger, cardamom & cinnamon sticks. Check for sweetness and add more agave if you desire. Let the tea mixture steep for about 10-15 minutes. Strain the tea, stir in the condensed milk and cool the tea down completely. Serve over ice, garnish with mint.

Iced Chai Tea

There was a time when I went to this famous coffee house to get this yummy drink hot or cold. Well, it wasn't too difficult to figure out the ingredients. I love the warm, spicy flavors of this tea and the soy milk adds depth and sweetness to this delicious drink.

10 cups of water
10 black Chai tea bags
½ cup sugar or sugar substitute

1 pint of vanilla soy milk or almond milk
3 oz of sugar-free vanilla syrup
Light whip cream (optional)

Bring the water to a boil, turn off the heat and add the tea bags to the pot along with the sugar. Let the tea bags steep for about 10-15 minutes. Remove the tea bags and cool the tea down completely. Add the tea to a large pitcher and stir in the soy milk. Pour in glasses and garnish with whipped cream.

Cook's note: you can also serve this hot. Follow the same instruction, but do not cool down.

Fizzy Pom (non-alcoholic)

The mix of citrus and pomegranate juice is so tasty and refreshing. The pomegranate juice is loaded with plenty of antioxidants, and the citrus beverage gives it that fizzy, tingly feeling on your lips.

16 oz citrus beverage
16 oz 100% pomegranate juice
1 cup of ice

4 martini glasses
½ cup of sugar
Lime wedges, plus some for garnish

Add the citrus beverage and pom juice to a large pitcher and stir; add the ice and stir once more. Rub each martini glass rim with a lime wedge and dip each glass in sugar, making sure the rim is completely coated. Divide the fizzy pom beverage between the glasses and garnish each with a lime wedge.

Pom Mimosa

This is my take on the traditional mimosa. I love the tang of pomegranate juice and the sparkling wine adds a little something special to the cocktail.

Equal parts:
100% pomegranate juice
Sparkling wine (I use Prosecco)

Add the ingredients to a large pitcher chill and serve.

Mock Rita (non-alcoholic)

The drink is great for non-drinkers, pregnant ladies, and even the kiddos.

Equal parts:
Cranberry juice
Lemon-lime soda or sparkling flavored water
Sugar (to taste)
Champagne glasses
Maraschino cherry for garnish

Add the cranberry juice and lemon-lime beverage to a large pitcher and stir; add the ice and stir once more. Rub each champagne glass rim with a lime wedge and dip each glass in sugar, making sure the rim is completely coated. Divide the Mock Rita beverage between the glasses and garnish each with a maraschino cherry.

Blue Haze

Fruity, frothy and delicious is how I would describe this yummy cocktail.

3 cups Hypnotic alcoholic beverage
½ cup pineapple juice
1 cup of ice
4 martini glasses
Maraschino cherry and pineapple chunk for garnish

Add the Hypnotic, pineapple juice and ice to your blender. Blend until well incorporated and frothy. Drop one cherry into each glass and divide the cocktail evenly between the glasses. Garnish the side of each glass with a pineapple chunk

Purple Passion

This is great for ladies' night or any night really. Easy to make and smooth going down.

Equal parts:
Vodka
Triple sec
Fill shaker with ice
Grape juice
2 – 6oz glasses

Add vodka and triple sec to shaker; give it a few shakes and pour evenly into glasses. Top off with the grape juice. You can serve straight up or on the rocks.

Cook's note: a jigger equals 1 oz or a shot

Raging Rita

This is a great signature cocktail for your next get-together.

½ can of sugar-free Red Bull energy drink
Equal parts lemon-lime margarita mix
1 jigger of silver tequila

Stir all ingredients together and serve on the rocks. Garnish with lime wedges.

Cook's note: a jigger equals 1 oz or a shot (feeling a little brave? Double the shot if you dare.)

Buttery Scotch

Creamy and buttery; it tastes so much like a dessert, you'll forget you're having a cocktail.

1 jigger of Bailey's Irish Cream
1 jigger of Butter shots liquor
Whipped cream for garnish

Fill the shot glass halfway with 1 jigger of Bailey's Irish Cream and 1 jigger of butter shots liquor. Garnish the shot with whipped cream. Repeat the process for the number of shot glasses you have.

Cook's note: a jigger equals 1 oz or a shot (feeling a little brave? Double the shot if you dare)

Innocent Envy (non-alcoholic)

Innocent because it's alcohol-free, yet it's green with envy. Enjoy.

½ can sugar-free Red Bull
Lemon-lime Margarita mix
Mint leaf (for garnish)

Pour the Red Bull in a tall glass. Top off with lemon-lime Margarita mix. Serve on the rocks and garnish with a mint leaf.

Recipes
A - Z

CPSIA information can be obtained
at www.ICGtesting.com
Printed in the USA
LVIC061045150920
664995LV00005BA/51

* 9 7 8 1 7 1 0 5 7 1 5 6 1 *